AN AMISH CHRISTMAS WISH

and

The Christmas Prayer

Bonus short story

WRITTEN BY
Samantha Jillian Bayarr

BONUS
Amish Sugar Crème Pie
Recipe

Also by Samantha Jillian Bayarr

Jacob's Daughter Amish Collection
Jacob's Daughter
Amish Winter Wonderland
Under the Mulberry Tree
Amish Winter of Promises
Chasing Fireflies
Amish Summer of Courage
Under the Harvest Moon

Amish Romance
The Quilter's Son
An Amish Christmas Wish

Amish Love Series
An Amish Harvest
An Amish Courtship
An Amish Widower
Amish Sisters

LWF Amish Series
Little Wild Flower Book I
Little Wild Flower Book II
The Taming of a Wild Flower
Little Wild Flower in Bloom
Little Wild Flower's Journey

Christian Romance
Milk Maid in Heaven
The Anniversary

Christian Historical Romance
A Sheriff's Legacy: Book One
Preacher Outlaw: Book Two
Cattle Rustler in Petticoats: Book Three

**Please note: All editions may not be available yet.
Please check online for availability.**

CHAPTER 1

I will search for the lost and bring back the strays. I will bind up the injured and strengthen the weak...
Ezekiel 34:16

"Move, you stupid car! I don't want to be stuck here another minute!"

Grace Fisher rocked the car from forward to reverse, and then back again. It wasn't going anywhere in this blizzard. She was stuck in the ditch only inches from a large tree where her car had slid off the icy road. Snow swirled in thick patches in front of her, making it impossible to see farther than the hood of her car. Her wipers moved slowly across her windshield, chunks of icy snow weighing them down.

Shivering some from fear and some from the cold, Grace picked up her cell phone and tried to make a call. No service; she wasn't surprised. She was so far from civilization she was surprised she was still in Elkhart County. Leaning her head over the edge of the steering wheel, she began to sob. How had she managed to let her life get so out of control?

Grace rolled her hand over her protruding tummy, relieved when she felt the familiar *thump-thump* of her *boppli* kicking. Her *daed* had taken one look at her middle, and told her not to return without a husband, and *not* until she'd made a full confession. How was she going to get a husband now? No *mann* in the community would have her; the sins were all too evident. Since she wasn't a widow; she was a shame to her family, and she had been shunned after leaving the community the day after her baptism. It wasn't long after that she married and became pregnant, making it impossible for her to return to the community—especially since she was now divorced.

Before she left the community, Grace had panicked as soon as she'd taken the baptism. All she'd seen at the time for her future was being married to Ethan Bontrager—a *mann* whose proposal she'd turned down. It wasn't that Ethan wasn't a *gut mann,* because he was. Ethan was everything she'd ever wanted, but she'd always thought of him as more of a *gut* friend. Grace had never been certain she loved Ethan enough to be his *fraa* since she'd never experienced the outside world during her *rumspringa*. Well, now she had, and the world had not been kind to her. Even as regret tried to creep into her thoughts, she realized if she'd accepted Ethan's proposal, she wouldn't have her *boppli*—and that was *not* something she would ever regret—even if she *was* facing the possibility of having to give up the *boppli* for adoption. Tears blurred her vision at the thought of her *boppli* being raised by someone else. Her *familye* had been her last hope, and Ethan Bontrager was so far in her past, there was no looking back.

No sense in borrowing more trouble. Surely Ethan is married to another by now; he had been the most handsome of the menner in the youth group.

The fact remained, she was now alone, pregnant, and stuck in a blizzard. That one mistake in judgment had left her to deal with a pregnancy on her own. Grace had been abandoned by the baby's father, who had divorced her only three weeks after marrying her. By the time she'd discovered she was pregnant, he'd already taken up with another woman and denied having part in it. Grace had shouldered the responsibility on her own, taking a job at a diner. She'd rented a small studio apartment in town, but when she could no longer do her job effectively, the manager had insisted she take her maternity leave. With no paycheck, she'd lost her apartment and decided her only option was to go home. Returning to the community had been her last hope. But now, even that was gone.

Grace flipped on her hazard lights, but who was she kidding? No one was going to find her out here in this blizzard. She knew she might be stuck for the night and was suddenly thankful she'd had the presence of mind to fill the gas tank. At least she wouldn't freeze to death as long as the heater held out. Her car was twenty years old and rusted beyond recognition, but at least it got her where she needed to go—until now. She could only hope that when the snow let up, she'd have cell service again and could call for a tow truck.

Her stomach rumbled with hunger. Grace hadn't eaten anything all day, and when she'd shown up on her *daed's* doorstep, she'd smelled the meal her *mamm* had been cooking. The aromas coming from her *mamm's* kitchen had put a lump in Grace's throat. Grace hadn't seen her, but she could envision the woman's routine as if she was watching it in person.

Her *daed* had not let her past the kitchen door, and Grace knew it was his duty to protect his *mamm* from outside influences that would shake her faith.

But Grace couldn't understand how a parent could turn away his own flesh and blood—especially now that she was about to have a *boppli* of her own. Grace missed her *mamm,* but she hadn't missed the stern ways of her *daed* or the *Ordnung.* The look of disappointment on her *daed's* face now imprinted in her mind, Grace determined she had been temporarily *narrish* to think that coming back to the very community that had turned its back on her was a *gut* idea. She'd convinced herself that if her parents took her in, she could keep her *boppli,* but even that hope was lost.

Her stomach rumbled again at the thought of her *mamm's* cooking. She wasn't certain her nervous stomach would keep any food down, but she needed to eat for the sake of the *boppli.* Knowing there was food in her bag in the trunk, Grace pulled the trunk latch and pushed open her reluctant car door. One foot out, and she knew just how slippery the road was. It didn't help matters that she was dizzy from not eating all day.

Heavy snow assaulted Grace as she stepped slowly to the back of the car. The wind swirled around her, pulling open her coat that no longer closed around her ample middle. One strong gust flapped her coat violently, causing her to lose her footing. Grace reached for the side of the car, but it was slick with snow. Her legs crumbled beneath her, sending her down onto the icy, country road. Her head hit the ground, the snowflakes hitting her cheeks turning to a white haze as her eyes drifted closed.

If only she hadn't made that Christmas wish…

CHAPTER 2

The Lord is my rock, my fortress and my deliverer. My God is my rock, in whom I take refuge.
2 Samuel, 22:2,3

Ethan closed the barn door, shielding himself from the snow that whipped across his face, stinging his already cold cheeks. In the thickness of the falling snow, he thought he heard the faintest of noises. It sounded almost like spinning tires of an *Englischer's* car. Ethan had heard that sound before. His cousin, Henry, had hidden a car during their *rumspringa,* and so Ethan knew the sound well. He himself had gotten that car stuck in the snow when Henry had urged him to drive it. After that experience, Ethan was cured of any curiosity concerning cars. He was content to keep the slow pace inside the *familye* buggy.

The main road was just over a half-mile hike from the *haus,* and he feared walking all that way in the blizzard, only to find nothing when he got there. He knew that checking to see if someone needed help was the right thing to do, but the snow was already several feet deep and drifting even higher in the wind. He would be snowed in within the hour if the weather didn't let up—sooner if it got any worse.

Ethan was content knowing that his *familye* was safely in Nappanee by now visiting his *aenti* and *onkel.* This would be his first Christmas without his *familye,* but he'd elected to stay behind and care for the animals. His *mamm's bruder* had fallen ill, and so his *mamm, daed,* and younger *schweschder* had left three days ago to visit, knowing they would stay over during the Christmas holiday. Ethan had his older *schweschder* only five miles away, but if this weather didn't let up, he'd be spending the holiday alone.

Turning from the noise, Ethan gathered another armful of wood from the wood pile and began to take it into the *haus.* It was nearly dark, and he wanted to get the chore done so he could settle in for the night. The animals were snug in the barn, and he'd blanketed each of them and given them extra hay in their stalls. Even the barn cats were snug in the hayloft after enjoying their meal. With everything taken care of, Ethan was more than ready to get out of the cold and under a warm quilt, with nothing but a blazing fire and a cup of *kaffi* to keep him warm for the remainder of the night.

Surveying the pile of wood just inside the mudroom, something prompted Ethan to go back outside to get just one more bundle for the sake of precaution. He didn't want to trek all the way back to the side of the barn for another armful, but he felt the sudden urge to go back out once more. Pulling his scarf up over his face, Ethan shouldered out the kitchen door. On the icy step, he slipped, causing him to grab the railing. When he looked up, he saw faint flashing lights from the main road. He said a quick prayer, and felt the prompting even stronger. Whoever was down there needed his help.

Ethan pulled down his hat to shield his eyes from the icy snow. Taking shorter strides in the knee-deep snow helped to keep him from falling. The snow was so thick and wild as it blew that he could scarcely see in front of him at times. The snow had drifted in some spots that were nearly as tall as he was. The closer he came to the road, he spotted a car. The driver's side door was open and so was the trunk. The car appeared to be abandoned. Had the owner gone looking for shelter in this storm? If so, then why was the car still running?

Walking around the front of the car, Ethan spotted someone on the ground.

It was a woman!

Had she been hit by a passing car? Covered in snow, she was as lifeless as a frozen corpse lying on the road. Bracing himself against the side of the car,

Ethan went to her, praying she was still alive. Kneeling down beside her, relief washed over him when he noticed the faint puff of warm fog streaming steadily from her nose.

She was still breathing!

Brushing the snow from her cheeks, his heart nearly gave way when he looked into her familiar face.

It was Grace Fisher—and she was pregnant!

Her lips were blue and her cheeks severely chapped from the wind and snow that had settled there. How long had she been lying here? Pushing down his shock, Ethan stood up and grabbed her keys out of the ignition, closed the car door and the trunk, and stuffed the keys in his coat pocket. Then he pulled off his scarf and wrapped it around Grace's head, her frozen hair thick with snow.

Scooping Grace up into his arms, Ethan was determined to carry her the half mile back to the *dawdi haus* where he was living. If his *daed* had been home, he'd have gone back to the *haus* to get a horse and cart, but he couldn't leave Grace here alone. If his *daed* had been home, he knew the *mann* would make him take Grace back to her *vadder's haus,* and he was momentarily thankful his *daed* was *not* there. But judging from the direction her car was pointing, he imagined she had just come from there. And from the size of her mid-section, he'd also guessed that her *daed* had turned her away. Grace had been shunned when she'd left the community after her baptism. Did she have an *Englisch* husband somewhere that was missing her? But if she did, what was she doing at her parent's *haus* on such a stormy night? Was it possible that the *boppli* was conceived out of wedlock? He hadn't seen a ring on her finger, but that didn't mean anything since Grace was Amish, and the Amish didn't wear rings.

Ethan pushed the accusations from his mind as he struggled to put one foot in front of the other. Grace was a thin, frail, wisp of a woman, but with the added girth of the *boppli,* she was awkward in his arms.

Trying to retrace the path he'd made in the deep snow on the way down the driveway, it was difficult to see more than a foot or so in front of him. He now wished he'd had the forethought to bring a lantern so he could find his way back to the *haus*. Was he even going the right direction? It was almost too dark now to see, even if the snow wasn't a hindrance. His previous steps had been filled in with drifting snow, and each step he took seemed to take him longer to make. He cradled Grace against his chest and ducked his head against the wind and ice that sliced across his cheeks like razorblades.

Where was the *dawdi haus?*

Gott, please light the way and guide my steps to keep me on a straight path. Shelter us in your arms and lead us back to the shelter of the dawdi haus.

Within seconds, his foot ran into something. It was the large rocks at the end of the driveway that his younger *schweschder,* Miriam, had thought was a nice addition to his *mamm's* flower garden. He'd tripped over them and complained about them so many times, he knew exactly what his foot had run into. Suddenly grateful for Miriam's garden rocks to mark his location, Ethan knew that if he turned to the right, the *dawdi haus* was only a few short steps away.

CHAPTER 3

A wise man has great power, and a man of knowledge increases strength.
Proverbs 24:5

Ethan tossed another log on the fire, tempted to stay near the hearth to warm himself, but he had to get Grace warmed up first. He'd pulled off her boots and wet socks, checking for signs of frostbite. Then he replaced them with a pair of his own socks that were clean and dry, and then wrapped her icy hair in a clean towel. But even the extra quilts would not be enough to get her warmed quickly enough.

Then he had a brilliant idea.

Throwing his coat back over his shoulders and tucking his hat low on his head, Ethan braved his way out to the driveway to retrieve Miriam's garden rocks. If he warmed them in the fire, he could place them at the end of the bed to warm Grace's feet and hopefully ward off any frostbite. While he was out there, he would go to the barn and call the doctor for advice.

He was thankful he and his *daed* had put a fresh coat of red paint on the barn over the summer, for, even in the densest of snow, he would be able to find it. Being able to see the white-washed *haus* when he returned was what worried him the most. Shuffling his feet to make a trail through the thick snow, Ethan slowly made his way to the barn. Once inside, the animals bellowed, meowed, and whinnied in protest against the gust of freezing air he'd brought in with him. Ethan stomped his feet toward the workbench where the phone rested. As he picked up the handset, relief washed over him at the sound of the dial tone. Like everyone in the community, Ethan knew Doctor Davis' number by heart. When he picked up on the fourth ring, Ethan talked as fast and to the point as possible, not wanting to be away from Grace any longer than was necessary. Grabbing a pen, Ethan wrote the instructions, knowing he was not in a state of mind to remember everything the *mann* was telling him.

Soon Ethan was tucking the notes into the pocket of his trousers and shouldering his way out into the blizzard once again. Standing with the barn door at his back, he knew that Miriam's garden rocks were to his left, and once he retrieved them, the *dawdi haus* would be at his back. Making a mental note of the directions he needed to turn, Ethan trudged through the snow that didn't seem as deep only a few minutes before. He retraced his footsteps toward the *dawdi haus* until the large oak tree was directly to his left. The branches were illuminated against the light of the battery-operated lantern, exaggerating the fierceness of the snowstorm.

Icy snow pelted Ethan's face, stinging his eyes, as he struggled against the wind. He had to make it to that tree and back to the *dawdi haus* for Grace's sake—for the sake of her *boppli.*

Gott, don't let me lose my way. Reach down and place a hedge of protection over me, and keep Grace safe while she's in the dawdi haus alone.

Though Ethan was numb, he was determined to get those rocks that he knew could help warm her up. He'd loved her since they went to school together, but she'd never shown him anything other than deep friendship. He'd always hoped he'd marry her, but when she'd left the community, he'd put that hope to rest. Now, she belonged to someone else, and she was going to be a *mamm.* Grace had a *familye*—something he'd always thought *he* would have with her.

Just past the tree, Ethan ran into the rocks again with his feet. *Bless you dear schweschder,* he thought as he nudged at three of the rocks that were nearly twice the size of softballs and cradled them close to him. Turning completely around, Ethan prayed the *dawdi haus* was still behind him, and he hadn't gone off course. Holding the lantern up in the darkness, the light illustrated the squall of the storm.

In the blackness, Ethan prayed he would find his way through the short distance to the *dawdi haus* where Grace lay unconscious waiting for him—even if she didn't know it. Should he have called her *daed?* Ethan wondered if it would have mattered if he had. He knew Grace was shunned, and he was risking a lot by having her in his company. But that didn't matter to him at the moment, for his heart would not allow him to turn her away. Was it wrong for him to hope she didn't have a husband? Even though it had only crossed his mind for a brief moment, he knew he should likely repent for such an impure thought.

He would include it in his prayers later. For now, all he cared about was getting back to Grace.

CHAPTER 4

Faith is being sure of what we hope for and certain of what we do not see.
Hebrews 11:1

Ethan had to remind himself that Grace was not his *fraa* as he tucked the warm stones under the quilts at the end of his bed where Grace was resting peacefully. She'd stirred a few times, but she hadn't opened her eyes. She was supposed to be *his fraa*.

Was it too soon to believe that *Gott* had answered his prayers? It was his one wish for Christmas—to have a *familye* of his own. But with no prospects, and being snowed in with a pregnant woman, it wasn't looking hopeful for him since Christmas was only days away. Nonetheless, Ethan dared to dream such a thing, though he was certain he had no right to. For the first time in his life, Ethan realized what it meant to have faith the size of a mustard seed.

Ethan gazed upon the woman in his bed, watching the gentle rise and fall of her chest, and taking comfort in knowing that she was still alive. In the dim lantern light, her beauty nearly took his breath away. He had missed her; that he was certain of. He wondered if she had thought about him since she'd been gone. Guessing from the *boppli* she was carrying, he'd have to say no. She'd turned down his proposal before, but if she was alone, would she turn him down again? No sense in borrowing more trouble until he knew what her situation was, and he wouldn't know that until she woke up.

Doctor Davis had told him that she would probably sleep through the night, but he was to try to wake her every hour or so. She'd stirred a few times, and the doctor had said that was a *gut* sign she was recovering from the trauma of her fall. It was the *boppli* that Ethan was most concerned about. Per the doctor's instructions, he'd placed his hands around her belly to feel for kicking, and so far, he was grateful for those little kicks he'd felt. It was a tiny miracle, and Ethan felt joy at those kicks as though they had come from his own *boppli.*

Ethan lifted the towel from Grace's head since the ice had melted from her hair. Still damp, her blond tresses fell across her shoulders. A sigh escaped her lips that were no longer blue, but had turned a soft rose color that complimented her pallid complexion. If Ethan wasn't careful, he could get lost in her beauty, wishing for things he had no right to wish for.

No longer shivering, Grace had calmed to a peaceful state, and Ethan wondered if the woman he'd loved was still in there somewhere. He steeled his emotions, guarding his heart against further heartbreak from the woman that lay in his bed. If it was possible, he would keep his distance except to care for her and nurse her back to health. The storm wouldn't last long, and she would be out of his life again, and he was not willing to let her absence leave another scar on his heart.

Anna Yoder had shown some interest in him at the Christmas singing, and he would keep his mind on the possibility of a future with her. Sadly, a piece of his heart would always belong to Grace, but he had to move on. It was evident that Grace had moved on, and Ethan was determined to do the same. He would not allow himself to fall in love with her all over again, only to suffer another heartbreak when she left the community a second time. She had a life outside of the community—among the *Englisch*. At least now he would finally have the closure he'd needed for more than a year since she'd left.

Ethan walked into the main sitting room toward the kitchen. He needed to warm up his *kaffi*. He was still pretty chilled from going to the barn and getting the stones to warm his bed for Grace. It was late, and he knew he should try to get some rest, but he would need to rouse her again shortly, so he hoped the *kaffi* would keep him alert enough to care for her. The doc had suggested setting his wind-up alarm every hour, but Ethan was certain he would not need it. His mind was so jumbled with conflicting thoughts, he wasn't certain he would be able to sleep as long as Grace was in his bed.

Placing his cup of *kaffi* on the fireplace mantle, Ethan held his hands out toward the crackling fire. He'd brought a rope in with him from the barn, knowing that by morning, the snow would be so thick, he would have to tie it from the back porch of the *dawdi haus* and then to the barn door in order to make his way back safely. He hoped it would let up, but it didn't seem like it had any intention of doing so. Ethan shivered as he listened to the wind howl, thick snow already drifting halfway up the windows. There was no doubt about it; they were snowed in.

CHAPTER 5

Find rest, O my soul, in God alone; my hope comes from Him. He alone is my rock and my salvation; He is my fortress, I will not be shaken.
Psalm 62:1,2

Ethan startled. Nearly falling off the chair he'd placed beside his bed, he reached for the alarm clock and pushed the *off* button. He shivered a little and knew the fire had probably died down while he'd slept. Outside, the wind continued to howl, the snow pelting the windows. Standing over his bed, he watched Grace breathing for a minute, grateful she was still with him.

Trying not to worry about the weather, Ethan went out to the sitting room to stoke the fire. His supply of wood was growing low, and he would need to gather more as soon as morning light broke. For now, he was content to bask in the warmth of the hearth. Once the fire was blazing again, Ethan went to get the stones to reheat them. He didn't want Grace to shiver in the cold room.

Ethan could feel the temperature change as soon as he entered his bedroom. He opened the door wide to let the heat from the other room enter as he approached his bed with caution. Lifting the quilts, Ethan snatched the stones from the foot of the bed and carried them to the fireplace. Using the large tongs, he gently placed each of the stones in a position to maximize their exposure to the flames that licked the logs. This time, they did not sizzle when he placed them over the flames. They had sufficiently dried out the first time.

While he waited for the stones to heat up, Ethan went to the adjoining kitchen and put on the kettle so he could clean the cut near Grace's temple. Doctor Davis had told him to change the dressing and clean it at least once during the night to ward off infection. He gathered some herbs from the cupboard to make a poultice. It wasn't deep, only a scalp wound, but Ethan determined to try to fix the little things he felt were more in his control.

With everything ready, Ethan went to his room to dress Grace's wound and try to wake her enough to make sure she hadn't slipped into a coma. He'd felt bad every time he'd tried to wake her, knowing she could probably use the rest, but that was the doctor's orders, and he didn't want to deviate from the instructions for fear something would happen to

Grace. First, he carried the hot stones in the folds of a thick towel and replaced them at the foot of the bed. Then he brought in the tea poultice so he could replace the makeshift dressing on Grace's head.

Setting the tray of supplies at his bedside table, he placed a gentle hand on Grace's shoulder and called out her name.

"Can you hear me, Grace?" He'd said it several times, but all she did was flutter her long lashes. When she let out a quiet groan, Ethan was satisfied he'd woken her sufficiently. He feared what was going to happen when she fully woke and discovered where she was, and with whom. What would he say to her? Would he have the courage to ask her about the *boppli* and her husband, or would she offer the information on her own?

Ethan tucked the back of his hand in the crook of Grace's neck to check for signs of fever. She was still pretty cool to the touch, so he knew he needed to do something more to warm her up. Pulling an extra quilt from the cedar chest at the end of his bed, Ethan took it to the kitchen and turned on the gas stove. Retrieving a large aluminum baking sheet, he placed it on the bottom rack of the oven and rested the quilt on it to keep it from scorching.

Standing at the kitchen sink, Ethan watched the snow hit the window. Frost had formed across the glass in a beautiful pattern that looked like wild plants growing along the surface. Only a small area remained untouched by the intricate motif—enough that Ethan could see just how deep the snow had become in the past few hours. It would be days before the snow plows would make their way out this far.

Panic seized Ethan when he wondered about the *boppli* Grace was carrying. How close to term was she? What if the spill she'd taken had caused some sort of harm that would force the birth before it was time? He would never be able to call for an ambulance in time, and the nearest midwife, though closer than Doctor Davis, was at least seven miles away. He suddenly wished his *mamm* was here. He was certain his *mamm,* who was a midwife, would not send Grace away in her condition, but his *daed* most likely would. His *daed* had not been as aware of his past with Grace, but his *mamm* and older *schweschder* had known all of it—right down to the refused proposal. At the time, Ethan had gone to Mr. Fisher and asked for his *dochder's* hand, and though he had consented, it had made no difference to Grace. She'd still turned him down and left the community. If she'd said *yes,* then that would be *his boppli* she was carrying.

CHAPTER 6

A house divided against itself will fall.
Luke 11:17

Grace felt like she'd bruised her entire body the way it ached. Her head pounded, and she felt nauseated worse than when she'd suffered morning sickness in her first trimester. As hard as she tried, she could not muster the energy to so much as lift her eyelids. Still in that twilight state of sleep, she tried to move, but she had sunken in the soft mattress beneath her. She didn't remember her bed ever being that soft. The sound of a crackling fire reached her ears, and the smell of burning logs tickled her senses. Was she dreaming? If so, could she make the nausea go away?

Warm hands clamped around her swelling abdomen. Who was touching her? A familiar voice spoke her name softly, as the hands prodded her stomach. She felt the gentle kicking of her *boppli*. She was somewhere safe—but where? Why was she so achy all over?

"Grace, are you awake?" the familiar voice asked her.

She parted her dry lips to answer, but no words escaped them. She wasn't able to move at all. Worry crept into her hazy thoughts. She was sore, but comfortable—what did that all mean?

"Grace, can you hear me?" the familiar voice called again.

She tried to nod, but wasn't certain if she had. She groaned a little, but even that hurt. Her throat felt a little sore. She shivered as she felt the blankets being pulled down away from her body. Then a warm blanket was placed on her and immediate heat radiated through her. She felt the weight of more blankets being piled on top of the warm one. The warmth relaxed her. Someone was taking care of her. It wasn't Jake; he'd been gone more than eight months. If not him, then who could it be? Who loved her enough to care for her and her *boppli?*

"I have some warm tea for you, Grace," the gentle male voice said. "Can you sip a little? The doc doesn't want you getting dehydrated."

Doctor? Was something wrong with her? Was she in a hospital? No, she was in someone's home, somewhere other than her parent's home.

When Grace felt the edge of a cup resting against her lips, a warm hand scooped behind her head and lifted. She swallowed a sip of meadow tea.

She was in an Amish home!

The cup tipped again, and she swallowed the familiar, warm liquid. It soothed her scratchy throat, and eased the nausea. She felt her head sink back into the soft pillow. The warm hand was gone. She drifted back to sleep to the sound of boots padding across hardwood flooring.

ଧ∽ଔ

Ethan felt sorry for Grace as she shivered when he'd unwrapped her to place the oven-warmed blanket over her. She was still in her wet clothes, but he didn't want to disrespect her by changing her into something dry. He hadn't grabbed any of her belongings from her car when he'd brought her back to the *dawdi haus.* When the sun came up, he would go into his parent's *haus* and borrow a dress from his *mamm.* The woman had packed on a little weight over the years, and her dresses were the only ones that would fit around Grace's abdomen. He would wait until she woke up to offer her the dry clothes. For now, all he could do was try to keep her warm so the damp clothing didn't cause her to catch a cold.

Ethan watched Grace settle back into a restful slumber, her shivering at bay for the time being. With her taken care of, Ethan left the room. Once in the sitting room, Ethan put another log on the fire, knowing that would keep them warm until first light. He stood over the hearth warming himself as his thoughts drifted to a time in his life when he'd been on top of the world—when Grace had been his.

Ethan had ignored the signs that had told him Grace was going to leave the community. Her interest when they'd gone through their *rumspringa* had become so overwhelming for her, especially since her parents had denied her that time that all her friends partook in. Her constant chatter about the *Englischers,* and wanting to wear her hair down, was something Ethan had become accustomed to. He'd not strayed too far from the community during his running around years, but Grace's *daed* was so strict with her, that he wouldn't allow her the freedom to make the choice on her own—he'd made it for her. For her, that meant no *rumspringa.*

When their time of *rumspringa* had worn down, and all the youth had begun taking the baptismal classes, Ethan had taken for granted that Grace was not ready to make that commitment. It was her *daed* who had pressed her into the decision instead of letting her decide for herself. He'd put so much undue pressure on her that she'd finally lost control of her life. She'd taken the baptism like a drone, and Ethan had begun to see the changes in her behavior. But he'd been brave enough to continue his relationship with her, hoping that when she became used to the idea of marrying and settling in the community, she would stop her constant talk of envy over the *Englischers* and their way of life. She'd called it *freedom,* but Ethan knew better.

The real freedom was in living a simple Amish life with *familye* by your side. He had seen first-hand how distant the *Englischers* were from their way of life. In his opinion, it was the best way to live. He'd never questioned his life in the community, but Grace had questioned everything to the point where she had hurt the people that loved her the most—especially Ethan.

Snapping out of his reverie, Ethan walked back into his room, circled to the other side of his bed and settled back into the chair, hoping he could get another hour of sleep before the sun came up.

CHAPTER 7

Pleasant words are a honeycomb, sweet to the soul and healing to the bones.
Proverbs 16:24

Ethan woke suddenly when his head rolled off the back of the chair and bobbed against his chest. Faint light peaked through the window that was covered up halfway with drifting snow. Heavy flakes continued to swirl, though the wind seemed to have died down a bit. Teeth chattering, Ethan stood and stretched, and then leaned over Grace. She was still sleeping, but she'd moved onto her side. That had to be a *gut* sign that she was on the mend. Deciding to let her rest for a little longer, Ethan prodded across the bedroom and into the sitting room. The fire was mere embers, providing very little heat into the small *haus.*

Shivering, Ethan gathered the last few splits of wood from the mudroom and staggered them over the embers in the bottom of the grate. He pushed at the coals until the logs ignited. Standing there for a minute watching the flames lick at the edges of the logs, Ethan made a mental list of the things he would need to do today. First up was taking care of the animals. While in the barn, he would make a call to Doctor Davis and report on Grace's condition. He knew it was not likely that the snowplows would make an attempt any further out than the main roads until this snow let up.

He suddenly wished he and his *daed* had fixed the runner on the sleigh. But without the parts, he would not be able to fix it on his own. Even with it fixed, he wasn't certain his gelding would make it through the deep snow. If Grace's condition worsened, he would make every effort to get her to a hospital; he would not let her down. In a rush of emotion, Ethan's throat swelled at the thought of something happening to her in this storm.

From the other room, Ethan heard the faintest of cries. He turned from the hearth and shouldered his way into the bedroom. Grace tossed about as though having a bad dream. He went to her and sat on the edge of the bed, taking her thrashing arms in his.

"Grace," he soothed. "You're safe. I'm here, Grace. It's me, Ethan. I won't let any harm come to you."

Calming down, Grace's brow relaxed, and a more peaceful look settled across her face. He could tell she'd heard him. The hand he'd been holding was still clenching onto him and tucked under her chin. Ethan didn't have the heart to let go, for fear he would disturb her. He sat watching her sleep, wondering what it would have been like had she married him. Several minutes later, she shifted position, letting Ethan's hand drop from her grasp. He was almost sad to let her go, but he had chores to tend to.

Inside the mud room, Ethan pulled on his boots, coat, hat, and scarf. He tucked his leather gloves and the rope under his arm and said a short prayer. With that done, he pushed his hands inside his gloves and opened the door slowly. Snow had drifted a few feet up the door, and some of it tumbled onto the linoleum. Not bothering to brush it out, Ethan stepped onto the porch and shuffled down the stairs. The wind threatened to rip his hat from his head, so he pushed it down over his ears. Ethan tied one end of the rope to the rail of the porch and looked out toward the barn that suddenly seemed farther away than it was yesterday. Stepping off the landing, Ethan sank mid-thigh in the deep snow. It was a struggle to lift each foot and take another step. Balancing was not easy, and he fell twice on the way to the barn. Now covered in snow, Ethan faced a new dilemma. The barn door was covered halfway up with snow.

Pushing at the snow in front of him, Ethan uncovered the handle. Tying the other end of the rope to the door handle, he gave the door a tug, hoping it would slide over enough for him to squeeze through. It barely moved. The iron track at the top of the door was covered in ice, preventing the door from sliding efficiently. Using his fists, he banged on the door, breaking some of the ice. Giving it another strong shove, it slid over enough for him make it through the opening.

Ethan closed the barn door against the wind. He could feel the snow down inside his boots, and his pant-legs were soaked nearly all the way up. He stomped his feet, trying to shake most of the snow from him, but it was pointless when he would be covered again on his return trip to the *dawdi haus.*

His gelding nickered an agitated greeting.

Ethan walked over to him and patted the side of his nose. "I'm sorry, King. I know I'm late getting your breakfast."

Ethan measured out a generous portion of grain from the feed sack and gave it to King as he patted his side. "That should hold you for a while." Ethan leaned in and nuzzled the gelding's ear. "Did anyone ever tell you that you eat like a horse?"

King bobbed his head and snorted as if to laugh at Ethan's joke. He let out a chuckle at his horse's attempt to lighten his mood. With King taken care of, the barn cats that had gathered at his feet would get his attention next.

At the back of the barn, Ethan opened the door to the chicken coop. Thankfully, he would not need to clean their roosts today since he'd replaced everything the day before. He filled their aluminum feeders and gave them fresh water from the sink. Gathering the eggs, Ethan couldn't help but think about the hot breakfast he would enjoy once he was safely back at the *dawdi haus,* and he prayed Grace would wake up to join him.

CHAPTER 8

Be sure you know the condition of your flocks; give careful attention to your herds.
Proverbs 27:23

"What's wrong with you this morning, Moo?"

Ethan patted the milk cow on her side as he set the pail below her to ready for milking. Her udder was extra full, most likely causing the cow some discomfort. He should have milked her last night, but he hadn't taken the time because of the weather.

"I'm sorry I didn't milk you last night, girl."

Moo shifted her feet impatiently, waiting on Ethan to relieve the uncomfortable swelling. She was nearing the end of her lactation and her milk supply was running low, otherwise she would have been worse off than she was. Talking to Moo to get her to relax, Ethan began telling the cow his troubles as though she could somehow help him to figure things out.

"I still love her, Moo," he said. "I can't help it. I think I will always love her, and that's why I didn't want to fix the sleigh. It was so I would have an excuse not to have to ask Anna for a sleigh ride after the Christmas singing. I didn't know Grace was going to come back here, but I've prayed about it. Do you suppose her being here could be an answer to my prayer?"

Moo let out a loud bellow, turning her head toward Ethan.

Chuckling, Ethan patted her side again.

"You're right. I should wait on *Gott* to direct me on that one. Do you suppose it's alright if I wish for her to be single?"

Moo looked back at Ethan and snorted.

"You're right. That isn't fair to Grace. Maybe I should call her *familye* and see if they know how I can get in touch with her husband."

Ethan finished the milking and put the pail up out of the way while he returned Moo to her stall. Picking up the phone, Ethan put it to his ear and heard nothing but static. He tried to dial out, but the line was dead. He wasn't surprised. The weight of the snow had probably brought down wires all over the county. Restoring the phone service would be second priority to getting the roads plowed, and he knew that wouldn't happen any time soon.

Grabbing the pail of milk off the bench, Ethan prepared himself to head back out into the blizzard. Breathing a quick prayer before opening the barn door, he braced himself for the cold and the wind. He was bundled back up, and the rope was secure. Getting back to the *dawdi haus* without spilling the contents of the milk pail would be another thing altogether.

Snow blew into the barn with such force when Ethan opened the door that it nearly knocked him off balance. He hoped the cheesecloth wouldn't blow off the top of the pail so the snow wouldn't water it down before he got it into the kitchen safely. He intended to warm some for Grace. She needed nourishment, and the milk would be *gut* for the *boppli.* There was a canister of cocoa in his pantry, and it would go nicely with the fresh eggs that dangled precariously in the basket hanging in the crook of his arm. The wind teetered the basket, but he tried to keep the handle steady. A hot meal would do both of them some *gut,* but not if he spilled it all on the way back to the *dawdi haus.*

Using the rope in his free hand, Ethan steadied himself the best he could while traipsing through the deep snow. In places, the drifts reached to his waist. He tried to retrace his steps, but the snow had blown across his path and filled in his previous footprints. With both his hands occupied, Ethan was unable to shield himself from the sting of the ice pelting his cheeks or the icy flakes that stung his eyes. The shock of the cold against his eyes, made Ethan blink uncontrollably, making it more difficult to see where he was going.

Up ahead, Ethan could finally see the *dawdi haus*. Eager to get inside and warm up, he tried to move a little faster. Milk sloshed out of the pail, disappointing him. He would have to be more careful, or he would lose all of it. When he reached the steps of the back porch, Ethan was very careful of each step, double-checking his footing on each one. Satisfied when he reached the top, he let go of the rope and reached for the door. Suddenly, Ethan lost his footing and fell forward, catching himself on the door, but he was not steady enough to keep the egg basket from dangling on his arm and spilling several of the eggs.

Frustrated, Ethan pushed open the kitchen door and set the milk pail on the floor of the mudroom, and then reached down to feel in the deep snow for the missing eggs. Unable to feel for them through his gloved hands, he pulled off his right glove with his teeth and stuffed his bare hand into the cold snow. Ethan smiled victoriously when he found one and stuck it back in the basket. Noticing another hole in the deep snow, he reached down and located another one. He could already see the yolks of two that had broken on impact, but after finding two more intact, he was satisfied enough to get back inside where it was warm.

Chilled to the bone, Ethan stepped inside the mudroom and began peeling off his wet clothes. Momentarily forgetting about Grace, Ethan walked toward his bedroom in his underclothes. He'd undressed in the mudroom at the end of each long work day ever since he'd moved into the *dawdi haus.* He was certainly a creature of habit.

Grabbing a towel from the washroom on the way there, Ethan threw the towel over his head and began to rub his wet hair. He walked into his room and went straight to the bureau without thinking, until he heard a sigh from behind him. Ethan panicked, not daring to turn around. Grabbing a clean pair of trousers, Ethan stuffed his legs into them as fast as he could. It wasn't an easy task since his skin was still damp, but with a lot of wiggling and tugging, he managed to get them up around his waist and fastened very quickly.

With his clean shirts on the pegs just a few feet from him, Ethan slowly turned around, relieved when he saw that Grace was still sound-asleep.

CHAPTER 9

Be joyful in hope, patient in affliction, faithful in prayer.
Romans 12:12

The smell of bacon and eggs invaded Grace's senses, but she couldn't be certain she wasn't dreaming it. Her stomach groaned from hunger, but she felt too weak to investigate the authenticity of the food. From what seemed like hours before, she'd been deep in a dream that she was married to Ethan Bontrager. She'd even seen him just as lifelike as possible walking across their room in his underclothes. But it wasn't a room she'd ever remembered seeing. Why would she dream something so brazen?

Ethan entered the room knowing he was behind schedule in checking on Grace, but he'd wanted to let her sleep just a little longer. He was certain she would likely wake up disoriented and maybe even frightened. Being in an unfamiliar place would make her nervous, and he couldn't imagine how Grace was going to react. He'd brought a tray of food into the room and set it on the bedside table, hoping she would at least see reason to filling her stomach. As far as he knew, she'd been more than fifteen hours without food. He was nervous about waking her, but it was time. His intention was to check on the *boppli* first so as not to worry her unnecessarily.

Placing a hand over Grace's abdomen, Ethan waited for the wee one to kick. Several minutes passed, and he felt nothing.

Gott, please wake this boppli so I know it's going to be alright.

At the conclusion of his silent prayer, Ethan swallowed a lump in his throat. Grace had come so far with the *boppli*, and Ethan didn't know how she would take it if something went wrong. Panicking, Ethan prodded Grace's abdomen with his strong hands, hoping the movement would set the *boppli* into motion.

"Move little *boppli*," *he said gently.*

Grace stirred, groaning slightly.

Ethan ignored Grace and continued to prod her stomach for a sign that the *boppli* was fine.

Grace opened her eyes, her hands instinctively covering over her abdomen to protect her *boppli*. She pushed Ethan's hands aside and sat up abruptly. Dizziness immediately consumed her, causing her head to flop back down onto the pillow. Her eyes closed, and the disorientation took her by surprise. She thought she was hallucinating when she'd seen Ethan. He was touching her stomach and talking to her *boppli!* Had she gone mad?

"Grace, are you awake?" Ethan asked. "I didn't mean to startle you. Open your eyes. It's me, Ethan."

Grace was frightened, but full of peace at the same time—confused would be more like it. If she opened her eyes and Ethan was not there, then that would mean she was hearing things that weren't there. But if he *was* there, well—why *would* he be there?

What had happened to her?

A dull ache in her head sent Grace's thoughts reeling. She had been in her car, stuck in a ditch. She'd nearly hit a tree—or had she hit it? Grace ran her hand over her abdomen. The *boppli* was still there, she'd felt it kick. But why would Ethan have his hands around her stomach feeling for the *boppli* unless he'd thought something was wrong?

Since he isn't really there, it shouldn't be a problem if I open my eyes.

Then she remembered.

She'd fallen in the snow near her car. She must have hit her head. She knew she was close to Ethan's farm when her car ran off the road. Had he found her and brought her back to his *haus?* Surely his *mamm* and *daed* would have sent her packing when they learned who she was. They wouldn't have thought she was an *Englischer*, and even if they had, they would not have taken her in. Unable to take the suspense a minute longer, Grace resigned to open her eyes and see for herself if the kind voice she'd heard belonged to Ethan Bontrager—the *mann* whose heart she'd broken just over a year ago.

Ethan waited patiently while Grace's eyelashes fluttered open. He was both eager to talk to her and apprehensive over seeing her again. Not that he hadn't spent time with her since she'd been here, but what had been one-sided was about to turn into a real conversation—he hoped.

"Grace, please open your eyes all the way. I want to talk to you. I've been wanting to talk to you since you've been here."

"How long have I been here," Grace whispered. Her throat was scratchy and dry, her voice raspy. "And where exactly is *here?*"

"I live in the *dawdi haus* on *mei daed's* property. You've been here with me since last night when I found you in the road near your car. I've been checking on your *boppli* every hour like the doc told me to, but I haven't felt it move yet this morning. Have you felt it kick?"

Grace tucked her legs under her as she rolled up on her side a little more. She rolled her hand over her stomach. "I just felt the *boppli* kicking. I feel achy."

Grace opened her eyes all the way and focused on Ethan. Was it possible that he'd gotten more handsome since she'd last seen him? His blond hair was pushed back off his forehead. It was wet. Had he just showered? Grace suddenly slapped her hands over her eyes. If she was really here with Ethan, then she had just seen him in his underwear!

CHAPTER 10

Be joyful always; pray continually; give thanks in all circumstances, for this is God's will for you in Christ Jesus.
1 Thessalonians 5:16-18

"What's wrong, Grace? Does your head hurt?"

Grace kept her face hidden from Ethan. "Were you just in here in your underwear?"

Ethan's face heated. "You saw that? I apologize for being indecent in front of you, but I was frozen to the bone and wasn't thinking about you being in my room. I've never had a woman in my room before."

Grace felt sorry for him. She could hear the embarrassment in his voice as it cracked with every word. But she was embarrassed too.

"I'm sorry. I shouldn't have said anything about it."

Grace felt Ethan's gentle hands take hers and ease them away from her face. "The important thing here is, how are you feeling?"

"I'm a little confused as to why I'm here in your room in the first place. I wasn't planning on coming to see you." Grace looked into Ethan's sudden sad expression and felt guilt overtake her. "I'm sorry for that—for everything. I should have given you an explanation before running off the way I did."

"You don't owe me any explanation."

Grace could see in his eyes that she *did* owe him an explanation. She'd messed up his life, her life, and her *boppli's* life with her bad decisions. She had no money and no place to go. She wasn't even sure *Gott* himself would bring her out of her troubles. One thing was certain; she would hide her shame from Ethan as best she could. She might not be able to hide her pregnancy, but she didn't have to admit to the shame of being a divorced woman.

Grace looked into Ethan's kind face wishing she could collapse in his arms and let him take away her troubles—even if only for a few minutes.

"What happened to me?"

"I found you down on the main road. I'm guessing you slipped on the ice. When I came upon your car, you were passed out on the ground. Your hair was frozen with ice, and you were real lucky you didn't get frost bite."

It all came back to her in a rush of memories. She shouldn't have gotten out of the car, but if she hadn't, Ethan might not have brought her here with him. Was her accident a blessing in disguise? She'd wished for a husband and *vadder* for her *boppli* for Christmas, and here he was—taking care of her the way a *husband* would. Grace's cheeks heated at her intimate thoughts. She was grateful for his care, but she knew he would not marry her in her condition.

Grace tried to get up again. Dizziness would not allow her to get out of the bed—Ethan's bed.

Ethan propped the pillows up behind her. "You aren't well enough to go anywhere yet. You stay put. I brought you some breakfast. You need to eat to build up your strength."

Grace eyed the tray of food Ethan had gestured to. Her stomach groaned at being so empty. She *was* pretty hungry. Perhaps with some food in her stomach, she would have the strength to be on her way—back to what, she had no idea.

Allowing Ethan to place the tray of food in front of her, Grace couldn't help but wish things could be different. He was truly a *gut mann*—unlike Jake, who'd left her with the responsibility to care for their *boppli* on her own.

Ethan helped Grace get started on her breakfast. All he wanted to do was take care of her. He'd wished for his own *familye* for Christmas, and he knew it was a long-shot, but he'd asked *Gott* for it anyway. If only Grace and her *boppli* could be *his*.

Grace picked at the food while Ethan sat quietly in the chair beside the bed.

"I'm certain you have better things to do than wait on me," Grace said quietly.

Ethan jumped up suddenly as though she'd startled him. "I do have some things I need to take care of. Will you be alright here for a little while?"

Grace nodded softly, enjoying his shyness. She watched him walk out of the room and felt a sudden loneliness in the quiet of the room. She took another bite of the eggs that were smothered in melted cheese just the way she liked them. Grace knew his kindness wouldn't last long. When she finished eating, she knew she would need to be on her way. She'd imposed on Ethan long enough. For him to take in a shunned woman would put him in jeopardy with the Bishop, and she did not want to be responsible for causing him trouble. She'd overstayed her welcome; she was certain of it. No matter how much she might want to stay, she had to go before she lost her nerve.

Ethan hated to leave Grace now that she had finally woken up. He'd wanted to stay and talk to her, but things had been awkward between them. He worried things would remain that way for however many days they were snowed in together. The thought of living in the same *haus* with Grace set fire to his thoughts. He still loved her, and he knew it would be difficult for him to keep from expressing those feelings to her, whether by direct or indirect admission. Surely she would pick up on his feelings toward her, and it would cause the situation to become even more awkward.

Ethan prayed for their friendship to remain intact. If nothing else, he intended to be a *gut* and supportive friend to her—no matter what happened or didn't happen between them. He feared her leaving without any resolve between them, but he put his trust in *Gott* to do *His* will.

CHAPTER 11

O Lord, be gracious to us; we long for you. Be our strength every morning, our salvation in time of distress.
        Isaiah 33:2

Ethan stomped the snow from his boots and shook himself out of his coat. The trip across the yard to his parent's *haus* and back had taken every bit of warmth from his bones. Leaving his clothes on this time, Ethan went over to the hearth and tossed a few logs into the fire. He stood over them, waiting for them to catch so he could warm up. He'd managed to get two dresses and an apron from his *mamm's* room, but he wasn't certain if Grace would accept the plain clothing she'd rejected when she'd left the community.

A faint thud from the bedroom drew him away from the heat of the fire and into his room. In the doorway, he spotted Grace standing near the bed, bending to pick up the plate of eggs that had spread across the braided rug that covered the majority of the wood floor. Ethan rushed to her side, grabbing the plate from her hands.

"Let me take care of that. You get back in bed. You need your rest."

Grace looked at his sincere expression, momentarily getting lost in it. "I have to go. I've overstayed my welcome."

Ethan clutched her elbow firmly, guiding her back up to the bed. "Even if you were well enough to *be on your way* as you say, we are snowed in. The snow has drifted as high as five feet in most places. I'm afraid you won't be going anywhere for the next few days until the snow plow comes around."

Panic seized Grace. "What do you mean we are snowed in? We can't be stuck here like this. What about your *familye?*"

Ethan tucked the quilt up to her neck to squelch her shivering. "*Mei familye* is visiting in Nappanee. They hadn't planned on being here for Christmas, as they were going to spend it there with my cousins. But they will most likely be staying on for an additional week until the snow is cleared away for safe travel."

Grace hadn't wanted to think about the holiday because that would mean that her wish had not come to pass, and that saddened her. "Tomorrow is Christmas Eve."

"Did you have plans for Christmas?"

Ethan watched Grace's countenance fall. "I had hoped for a taste of my *mamm's* sugar crème pie." Rolling her hand over her rounded abdomen, she added. "I don't think that wish is going to come true this Christmas."

Ethan didn't push the subject because he thought he already knew the answer. She had been shunned, and if she was married to an *Englischer*, her *familye* would not likely welcome her company for the holiday.

"I was going to visit with *mei schweschder* and her *familye* on Christmas, but the weather doesn't look like it's going to permit such a visit." Ethan looked out the window at the blowing snow. "It doesn't look like that snow is going to let up for a while."

Rubbing the stubble across his jaw, Ethan lingered near the window, hoping Grace would continue to talk to him, but she remained silent.

"I brought you a clean dress from the main *haus*. It belongs to *mei mamm,* but she wouldn't mind if you borrowed it," he said without turning around.

Grace didn't want to wear his *mamm's* dress, but she could hardly be ungrateful for the clean change of clothes. She remembered his *mamm* being a thick woman and figured the dress would fit around her abdomen.

"*Danki,* but I think I will wait a little while until the breakfast gives me the strength to change clothes."

Ethan didn't move from his spot at the window. "Do you remember when we were younger and winter storms like this were the highlight of the season?"

Grace smiled at the memories that suddenly flooded her mind of their school days. "It always meant the school would be closed. Then we would spend part of our day playing in the deep snow."

Ethan turned to look at Grace, sadness showing in his eyes. "When did we outgrow those days?"

Grace rolled her hand over her abdomen, avoiding Ethan's gaze. "We grew up, and our responsibilities shifted."

"When is the *boppli* due?"

"Next week. I pray this storm doesn't last much longer so I can get back home to deliver."

Why had she said that? She had no home to return to. She had no money and nowhere to go. She could only hope that she could stay here until she was ready to deliver. She would worry about where to go once they released her from the hospital. Reality had nagged her for the entire pregnancy, urging her to consider adoption. She had hoped that her *familye* would take pity on her and take her in so she could avoid losing her *boppli,* but that hadn't happened.

They had been her last hope.

Tears welled up in her eyes, causing her to turn away from Ethan. She could not bear the thought of having to give up her *boppli,* but with no job and no home, it was the right thing to do for the *boppli's* sake. Right now, she couldn't allow herself to think about giving birth, because it would only bring heartache she wasn't yet prepared to endure.

Ethan swallowed his fear and addressed the subject that had nagged him since he'd brought Grace to his *haus*. "I would offer to call your husband and let him know you are alright, but the phone in the barn is down from the storm."

"I'll call him when I get back on the road," she said quietly, trying to hide her shame.

There it was.

She had a husband.

Ethan felt crushed all over again—the same as he had when Grace rejected his proposal of marriage over a year ago. Without looking at her, Ethan padded across the floor of his bedroom and walked out the door. He couldn't bear to let her see his grief over her rejection a second time.

CHAPTER 12

Religion that God our Father accepts as pure and faultless is this: to look after orphans and widows in their distress and to keep oneself from being polluted by the world.
James 1:27

Grace rolled toward the window of Ethan's bedroom, looking out at the snow swirling angrily. She began to weep as she patted her abdomen.

"I'm sorry I messed things up for us," she said to her *boppli.* "If I'd made better choices, then I wouldn't be divorced and I wouldn't have to give you up for adoption."

Ethan's heart rolled against his ribcage with the force of the storm outside. He'd collapsed against the wall after leaving the room, and now he was sorry he had left Grace alone. How could he comfort her without revealing that he'd accidentally eavesdropped on her when she was clearly talking to herself and her *boppli?*

Ethan could hardly be happy that she was divorced when it was clear that she was suffering deep distress. But why would she consider giving up her *boppli?* And why had she led him to believe she was still married? Was it shame that had caused her to be secretive? Was it possible she'd visited her parents, hoping they would take her in, and they'd turned her away? She was so vulnerable and emotionally frail. He would give almost anything to be able to lift that burden from her, but he wasn't sure what he could do except pray for an answer.

Not yet ready to address the situation with Grace, Ethan tiptoed toward the front room so he could stoke the fire. The dilemma would take a lot of thought and a lot of prayer. Picking up the poker, Ethan stirred the coals as he stared at the small, windup clock on the mantle, wishing he could turn back time.

When they were younger, Grace had been so brave and sure of herself. The sizzle of the fire brought back a vivid memory of a younger Grace picking up a bee by its wings. Ethan had dared her to do it, and she'd complied as if it was second nature. But when the rest of the hive had swarmed toward them and they began to run through the woods, Grace had refused to let go of the bee in her fingers, fearful that it would sting her. When she'd finally let go, though they were racing through the woods running as if their lives depended on it, Ethan had never forgotten the confident smile she'd flashed him. It was that smile that he most wanted to see again, and he would do whatever he could to bring it back. Even if *Gott* did not mean for them to be together, Ethan was determined to take care of her and bring that smile back into her heart.

"Ethan," Grace called weakly from the other room.

Setting the poker back against the hearth, Ethan went to her, his heart heavy with love for her. As he entered the room, her back was to him.

He stopped short of the bed. "Did you need something?"

"I think I might need a little help getting to the washroom. I'm still pretty sore and a little stiff. I don't want to fall and hurt my *bop*..."

Grace didn't finish the sentence, and Ethan couldn't finish it any more than she could. He knew she must have been thinking it was no longer her *boppli,* and his heart ached for her.

"If you'd like, I can run a bath for you. I made sure the pilot light hadn't blown out in the storm. Sometimes the wind will blow it out, but I checked it this morning."

He was rambling, but he suddenly didn't know what to say to her. What do you say to a woman who is facing having to give up her own flesh and blood? He was afraid for her, but he didn't want to push her with an offer to care for her. He wanted to wait until he could talk to her a little more in-depth about the general subject. If it was within his power, he would take care of her, but he wasn't certain what the Bishop or his *daed* would have to say about that. No—he knew exactly what they would say. She was shunned—end of story. Unless she confessed, she would not be allowed to remain here in the community. Had she come back here to do just that?

"*Danki,* that is very kind of you. If you don't mind, I think I will wait here until the bath is filled. I think I may still be too weak to stand for too long."

Ethan left the room to fill the bath for her.

Is this what marriage would have been like?

More than anything, Ethan wanted to be married. He'd prayed for his own *familye* so much lately, he wondered if *Gott* was tired of hearing the same prayer from him. Now that Grace was here and she was not married, he wondered if he dared ask *Gott* to bless him with the opportunity to marry her. He was aware that *Gott* already knew his heart and what he would ask for before he even asked it, but he still feared asking. More than anything, he feared that *Gott's* answer would be *no.*

Ethan walked back into the room to assist Grace into the washroom. A warm bath would ease her physical aches, but he had a feeling the ache in her heart was still too fresh for him to interfere with. The last thing he wanted to do was to alienate her while they were closed in during this blizzard. What she needed and what she wanted were most likely two different things, and Ethan would not risk losing her all over again over another hasty proposal from him.

CHAPTER 13

For if you forgive men when they sin against you, your heavenly Father will also forgive you.
Matthew 6:14

Ethan carried a tray of food into his room for Grace. She was sleeping; the gentle sound of her breathing brought relief to him. She'd pulled her wet hair back in a conservative twist at the nape of her neck, and he wondered if she'd done it out of respect for him. He had not given her a prayer *kapp,* but he could see that she had fit nicely in his *mamm's* dress with plenty of room to spare. Grace was a mere slip of a woman, and if not for the tell-tale swell of her abdomen, she didn't show the pregnancy. His older *schweschder* had plumped up all over—especially in her face when she was pregnant with his nephew, but

Grace looked thin and almost frail as though the stress of her situation had affected her health. Still, she did possess that *glow* that most pregnant woman had, and it made her seem more lovely than he'd ever seen her.

Outside the window, the snow continued to swirl, though the wind seemed to have wound down a bit. The glass was nearly covered with a beautifully etched pattern of frost except for a tiny spot in the center where the sun seemed to have found earlier that day. The simple meal he'd prepared for the two of them would need to be enough to warm him and give him the energy to get through his evening chores. He'd stayed in most of the day, reading while Grace slept. He hated to wake her now, but she hadn't wanted to eat at the noon meal, and he didn't want her getting weak.

Setting the tray down on the bedside table, Ethan stood beside the bed for a moment, watching the gentle rise and fall of her breath. His arms ached to hold her and comfort her. Though she seemed to be sleeping peacefully, the crease in her brow would suggest she was under too much stress to relax. Lowering himself onto the edge of the bed, he bravely placed his hands over her abdomen to feel for the *boppli.* A smile spread across his face as the wee one bumped his hands.

Looking up, he was shocked to see Grace watching him. Standing up abruptly, Ethan cleared his throat to squelch the fire he felt creeping up his neck.

"Why is it every time I wake up you have your hands on my stomach?"

Despite her teasing tone and the smirk on her face, Ethan felt his face turn hot.

"I'm sorry. Doctor Davis told me to keep checking on the *boppli* and report any changes in activity to him."

"As long as it's doctor's orders," she humored him.

"It's a *gut* thing he's active because the phones are still down."

"What makes you think my *boppli* is a *buwe?*"

Ethan's face turned an even deeper shade of red. "They felt like *gut* strong kicks—like a *buwe*. But if that *boppli* is anything like its *mamm,* it's probably a spirited little *maedel.*"

Grace hadn't thought to want a *dochder;* she'd wanted to give her husband a son, but she didn't have a husband anymore. She had no husband to give a son to, and no *vadder* for her *boppli.* She was a mess.

Looking into Ethan's hopeful eyes made her desire to be his *fraa,* but she had no right to wish for such a thing. She had betrayed him more than a year ago when she'd left the community and then married the first *Englischer* who'd paid attention to her. Even though he hadn't acted bitter toward her since she'd been here, she could see in his eyes that he wished things had turned out differently for the two of them.

In all honesty, Grace wished for the same thing, but it was too late. She was about to have her ex-husband's *boppli,* and she would have to give it up for adoption. Her time with Ethan was limited, and she knew it was better for both of them if she was able to leave as soon as possible. Tears filled her eyes, and she couldn't look Ethan in the eye. She turned on her side facing the window again.

"I'll eat later," she sniffled. "Please leave me alone."

Ethan's heart sank at her words. He'd hoped she would talk to him, but the sadness in her eyes was evidence of her grief over the decision she'd made regarding her *boppli.*

"Is there anything I can do to help you, Grace?"

"*Nee,*" she whispered without turning around. "It's too late for Christmas wishes."

He wanted to pull her into his arms and tell her it wasn't too late, but he feared she would only reject him again. He could save her from having to give away her *boppli,* but Grace did not seem open to the idea despite the longing in her statement. Feeling discouraged, Ethan left the room as she had asked.

Her sniffles soon turned to sobs, and he couldn't bear to hear her cry. Ethan squared his shoulders and bravely walked back into his room. Sitting on the edge of his bed, he pulled Grace into his arms and held her head against his heart.

"I'm here for you, Grace. Let me help you."

"No one can help me," she sobbed.

Her warm tears seeped through his shirt, moistening his skin. It was enough to break his heart.

"Whatever it is, Grace, I'll try my best."

Grace shook under the force of her sobs. "I have already put you at risk by being here. I don't want to get you shunned too."

"You let me worry about that," Ethan soothed her. "Nothing is going to happen to me that isn't *Gotte's wille.*"

"I'm sorry I hurt you, Ethan."

He kissed the top of her head. "I forgive you, Grace—for everything."

CHAPTER 14

If you remain in me and my words remain in you, ask
whatever you wish, and it will be given you.
John 15:7

Grace woke up to the sound of icy rain pelting the window beside her. Except for that, the *haus* was too quiet. Dim light brought the room to life—a simple room, but one she had become very comfortable in—too comfortable. Pushing herself to semi-sitting, Grace leaned against the walnut headboard of Ethan's bed and propped the pillow behind her. Feeling stronger, she wondered if she should try to get out of bed on her own. With new pressure from the load her abdomen carried from the *boppli,* she was in dire need of going to the washroom and didn't think she could wait for Ethan's assistance.

Figuring he was most likely outside braving the weather to do his morning chores, Grace decided to swing her feet over the edge of the bed and test her strength. Her feet dangled, but no dizziness assailed her as she sat upright. She paused to say a quick prayer for strength, but feared she couldn't sit there any longer without wetting Ethan's bed. Not wanting to embarrass herself with such a thing, Grace slowly rose from the edge of the bed, holding onto the bedside table just in case.

Taking a step away, her feet seemed to remain steady as she waddled toward the washroom. Aside from a little stiffness, most of her aches had abated, making her walk confidently to her destination. It amazed her that such a simple thing could bring her joy. She had not wanted to depend on Ethan too heavily, worrying she would wear out her welcome.

৪৩

Ethan blew on his hands to warm them before beginning the milking. Moo was not a finicky cow, but she appreciated him warming his hands before touching her. He figured it was the least he could do for her since she was always so patient with him. She was like a part of the *familye,* just as much as the horses and barn cats. The chickens were a different story; Ethan was far too fond of fried chicken to become too attached to any of the stock, and there were too many of them to even try to tell them apart.

"*Gudemariye,* Moo, are you ready for your morning milking? I've got a *boppli* in the *haus* that needs some nourishment. I'm certain you remember Grace. She is resting inside and nearly ready to have her *boppli*. Do you think you could give us a little extra milk this morning?"

Moo bellowed and swished her tail in response.

Ethan patted her side. "*Gut* girl."

Letting his thoughts wander, Ethan envisioned the first time he and Grace had hidden in the barn loft, and the kiss they'd shared that day. It was a cold day, and she'd snuggled against him for warmth. It had been the perfect excuse to draw them together that day. He'd known from that very first kiss that he wanted to marry her. But he'd had no idea then that she would marry another *mann*—an *Englischer*.

৪৩৫৯

Grace looked at her reflection in the small mirror above the sink. She smoothed her hair back into place, and aside from the absence of a *kapp,* she suddenly looked very Amish. Was it possible that Ethan had seen the same thing when he looked at her? Or had he viewed her as an *Englischer?* Her mind momentarily wandered to what it would be like if she could turn back the hands of time and be Amish again.

Throwing warm water on her cold cheeks, Grace decided it was best not to wish for such a thing, even if it would take away the heartache of having to give up her *boppli*. She had to face the inevitable, but she would take it as *Gott* allowed. Her only real wish this Christmas was to avoid having to give up her *boppli,* and she still held out some semblance of hope that *Gott* would answer her prayer.

For now, she would concentrate on trying to repay the kindness of Ethan by going out to the kitchen and making him some *kaffi* for when he returned from his chores. As she walked past the hearth, she was delighted to see the large pine boughs and pinecones decorating the mantle. Sprigs of holly with bright red berries were tucked in-between the pine branches to give it just the right amount of color. The fire crackled and popped, and she paused to warm herself as she admired Ethan's holiday arrangement. The room was cozy, a single rocking chair tempting her to sit. A flash of herself rocking her *boppli* teased her, putting a lump in her throat—especially knowing Ethan had most likely made the rocker.

Jutting her chin and clenching her jaw, Grace shook the thought and padded toward the kitchen. She quickly located the *kaffi* and filled the pot from the sink. Scooping the aromatic grind into the basket, she assembled the percolator and set the pot on the gas stove. Striking a match from the box in the windowsill, Grace lit the burner, feeling satisfied she was able to accomplish such a small contribution.

While she waited for the *kaffi* to brew, she sliced two pieces of banana bread that she found on the counter under a piece of cheesecloth. She found butter in a covered dish next to it. After placing them on plates, she set them on the table in the corner. She located the sugar and put that in the center of the table, but she knew Ethan would bring in the milk.

The back door swung open, making Grace shiver from the deep chill that entered in with Ethan. The *kaffi* began to bubble up through the glass bulb on the top of the pot. Grace kept her back to Ethan as she turned down the burner and readied the cups.

Turning around, Grace handed a cup to Ethan. He took the steaming *kaffi*, his cold fingers brushing against Grace's warm ones. Warmth immediately filled him at the surprise, and he thought that this was something he could easily get used to.

CHAPTER 15

The Lord is good, a refuge in times of trouble. He cares for those who trust in him.
Nahum 1:7

Grace startled from a deep sleep when her *boppli* assailed her with a kick hard enough to nearly knock the wind from her. She sat up, the glow of the moonlight reflecting off the snow illuminating the room. Disoriented, Grace was relieved to see she was still in Ethan's room. From the window, she could see that the snow fluttered around, but not as heavy as the past few days. If the snow was letting up, then it was only a matter of time before the snow plows would make their way around the county, and she would have to leave the comfort of Ethan's protective presence.

If only Ethan could fulfill my Christmas wish.

Grace shifted in the bed, reaching for the windup alarm clock on the bedside table. It was nearly five-thirty, and she knew Ethan would be getting up soon if he wasn't up already. Swinging her feet over the edge of the bed, Grace leaned back with her hand in the small of her back and stretched. She was achy, but very much ready to get up. She intended to make *kaffi* for Ethan.

Though she knew her time with him was limited, it didn't stop her from wishing things could be different between them. Her arms ached to be around him, and she now realized too late that she really loved him.

Padding her way across the wood floor, Grace was extra careful when she came upon Ethan sleeping peacefully on the sofa. He looked uncomfortable there, but he slept nonetheless. She paused in front of him, watching him. Moonlight streamed across his face, chiseling out his strong features. Even with his eyes closed he was handsome, his kindness apparent even in his sleep.

Grace tiptoed to the kitchen and set about making the *kaffi* as quietly as she could. She had no idea if Ethan was a light sleeper, but she wasn't going to chance waking him before he was ready. She found the makings for the morning meal, and wondered if she should start that too. Not knowing Ethan's morning schedule, she opted for just the *kaffi* for now.

"*Gudemariye,*" Ethan said groggily behind her.

Grace nearly jumped out of her skin. She turned around to face Ethan, his blond hair disheveled, his eyes squinting in the lamplight. She bit her lower lip to keep from giggling. "You scared me. I was trying to be quiet."

Ethan yawned as he leaned against the sink and looked out the window at the falling snow. "I should have been up a while ago. I need to get out to the barn and make sure the animals are cared for. The cold makes them a little more hungry than usual."

She had offered to make him dinner the night before, but Ethan wouldn't hear of it. He'd insisted she sit at the table while he prepared it. He'd relented and allowed her to peel the potatoes, but she was energetic enough to make the entire meal this morning.

"Would you like something to eat before you go out there in the cold?"

Ethan raked his fingers through his hair and sighed. He knew better than to get used to having Grace there to greet him every morning, no matter how much he'd wished for it. "*Nee,* if you're hungry, feel free to eat. There are a few eggs from yesterday and banana bread left over. I wouldn't mind some of that *kaffi* before I head out."

Grace pulled a thermos from the shelf and filled it with hot *kaffi* for Ethan to take with him to the barn. She didn't want to eat breakfast without him. She could wait so they could take the meal together— a meal that she would cook for him.

Ethan smiled as she handed the thermos to him. More than anything, he wanted to pull her into his arms and kiss away the sadness she tried to hide from him. But he couldn't do that without letting her know that he'd overheard her secret. Besides, she would think his actions improper and would likely become angry with him.

With them snowed in for at least another few days, he didn't want to do anything that would put a strain on the remainder of her stay with him. Ethan didn't want to think about the time when she would have to leave. If he had his way, she would marry him, and he would raise her *boppli*. Somehow, he didn't see Grace agreeing to such an arrangement, but if he didn't at least ask, then he would feel guilty that she would have to give up her *boppli* for adoption. He'd wanted to ask her why she had turned down his proposal after knowing him all their lives only to marry a *mann* she couldn't have known more than a few weeks, but he would have to put his own hurt behind him for the time-being.

Grace pasted on a smile. As she gazed into Ethan's silvery-blue eyes, she felt mournful at the loss of the one true love in her life. If it was possible, she felt more love for him than she ever thought she could. But was it too late for them?

CHAPTER 16

Ask and it will be given to you; seek and you will find;
knock and the door will be opened to you. For everyone who asks
receives; he who seeks finds; and to him who knocks, the door will
be opened.
Matthew 7:7,8

Grace was suddenly full of energy, despite the nagging ache in her lower back. She gave the floors a once over with the broom she found in the mudroom, and was even tempted to scrub the floors, but she feared being able to get back up from the floor. The *boppli* seemed to have sprouted growth almost overnight. The weight of her protruding belly pulled at the muscles of her lower back, bringing twinges of pain as she moved about Ethan's *haus*.

She couldn't help but make the bed she'd been sleeping in and straightening the already clean room.

Then she folded the quilts at the end of the sofa where Ethan had slept. When she finished, she brought the quilt to her face and breathed in Ethan's scent on the intricately sewn fabric. It was a mixture of wood from the fire and a spicy orange scent she recognized from the homemade shaving soap in the washroom. She took another deep breath, remembering the same scent when he'd held her close the night before. She longed to be in the safety of his arms, but she had to be practical. She would be leaving in a day or two, and she would never again gaze upon Ethan's handsome face or hear the kindness in his voice.

Steeling her emotions, Grace reluctantly placed the quilt at the far end of the sofa neatly. She looked about the room for any other chore she could do to show how grateful she was to him for taking her in, but the small space was already very tidy.

Glancing at the clock on the mantle, Grace noted that Ethan had been in the barn for over an hour. He would return soon, and she intended to begin the meal. He would need something warm after making the trek between the *haus* and the barn. She'd watched as best she could through the frosted window while he struggled to keep upright in the deep snow, but she'd lost sight of him the closer he'd gotten to the barn. The snow was still coming down too thick for clear visibility, and she worried about him finding his way back.

Standing at the stove, Grace lit the burner and heated the iron skillet on low while she scrambled the eggs. She found a chunk of ham, cut two large slices off the bone and set them in the skillet to fry. Then she went about slicing the last of the banana bread and buttering it, placing the slices on the corners of each plate she pulled from the cabinet.

Looking out the kitchen window as she flipped the ham over to brown the other side, Grace noticed Ethan making his way slowly toward the *haus*. She hurriedly put the ham on the plates and poured the egg mixture into the pan. The eggs sizzled before she could grab a spatula from the drawer to stir them. By the time Ethan came inside and got his coat off, she would have the breakfast on the table.

She heard the back door open just as soon as she portioned out the eggs onto the plates, scooping more onto Ethan's plate.

Poking his head around the corner, Ethan sniffed the air and smiled. "Smells *gut*. I could smell food the minute I stepped onto the back porch. It set my stomach grumbling."

Grace was pleased she'd made him happy. She motioned for him to sit after he'd washed his hands. Setting the plates on the table in the same places they'd sat at the evening meal last night, Grace fussed over the linens and *kaffi* cups. Ethan set the pail of milk on the counter, poured two large glasses, and brought them to the table with him. He set one in front of Grace, flashing her a smile of satisfaction before sitting. Once secure in his chair, Ethan bowed his head for the prayer, and Grace followed suit.

"Bless this food that was so generously prepared for me. Watch over mei familye and please bless Grace and her boppli."

Grace's heart caught in her throat at the mention of her *boppli*. It was so hard for her to keep her focus on the meal before her as Ethan dove into his breakfast as though he hadn't eaten for days. She was pleased that she was able to do something for him, even though her heart ached to be his.

Putting his fork down on his half empty plate, Ethan grabbed the linen napkin and dabbed his mouth before taking a gulp of milk. "*Denki* for cooking. I guess I was hungrier than I thought I was. How about you? You've barely touched the little bit of food you put on that plate."

Grace looked him in the eye for the first time since she'd been there. She had missed those eyes and that smile. She'd missed hearing his voice and the kind tone in which he always spoke. There was no comparison between him and Jake. Jake had always been in a hurry and often sounded impatient. What had she seen in him? Freedom from her Amish heritage? If so, then why was she back here wishing she could rejoin the community? Was it only because she had no other option? Her only other option was to return to the *Englisch* world without her *boppli.*

"I'm not as hungry as you are. You've been busy working up an appetite."

"It looks like you've been busy in here too. I noticed you swept the floor and folded the quilts on the sofa. Not to mention preparing this meal for me.

Should you be working so hard after the spill you took out there?"

Grace swallowed a sip of milk. Oh, how she'd missed fresh milk and eggs! "I feel fine except for the ache in my lower back, but that's to be expected since I'm so close to term."

Ethan looked at Grace then with an amusing look. "You and I are best friends. Why are we wasting time with this small talk?"

CHAPTER 17

Give to the one who asks you, and do not turn away from the one who wants to borrow from you.
Matthew 5:42

Grace had insisted on making the evening meal for Ethan to show appreciation for taking her in during the storm and taking care of her after her fall. She wished he'd had the ingredients to make a sugar crème pie, but his pantry lacked brown sugar and cinnamon. Asking Ethan to make the trip to the main *haus* in the cold on the chance that his *mamm* would have the ingredients wouldn't be fair to ask. Grace resolved herself to the fact that this Christmas would be without sugar crème pie, and it would be the first since she was old enough to eat it.

Knowing she had bigger things to concern herself with, Grace moved about the tiny kitchen preparing the most grand meal possible to celebrate the holiday. Despite her increasingly aching back, Grace was eager to spend some time with Ethan who'd spent the majority of the day out in the barn. She hoped he wasn't avoiding her, but she suspected he felt awkward around her now that she was awake and taking over his *haus.*

෨෬

Ethan hoped the cradle he fashioned would not upset Grace. He'd made several for women in the community, including his own *schweschder.* He had been making furniture since he was twelve, and had made enough of the cradles to finish in only a few hours. Knowing Grace's plans for her *boppli* made him wonder if it was *Gott* who had prompted him to make the cradle to change her mind about giving it up, or if it was his own selfish hopes that had put the idea in his head. Either way, Ethan hoped to change her mind and convince her to marry him and let him raise the *boppli* as his own. He knew it would have to be in *Gott's* timing when he asked her, and he was determined to wait on *Gott.*

Ethan had prayed for this one Christmas wish, and he'd had no idea how *Gott* would pull off such a miracle on such short notice. But he had faith that such a thing was possible. The only problem that he saw was that Grace seemed determined to leave, and he feared never seeing her again once the roads were clear enough for her to be on her way. Did he have the guts to ask Grace to marry him? Would a proposal make her stay, or would she run from him again?

෨෬

Grace sat down at the little table in the kitchen and sipped a cup of meadow tea. It warmed and calmed her as she realized her aches were most likely caused by overdoing it so soon after her fall. Though she was determined to finish the meal for Ethan, she knew better than to be on her feet too long—the ache in her lower back a reminder. Grateful that he wasn't inside watching over her, she mentally planned out a few things she wanted to say to him. For one, she knew she could not leave without telling him she still loved him, but she feared her present condition would turn him away from her. She'd led him to believe she was married, and it would be inappropriate for her to declare her love for him. But that was something she had to decide if she was willing to risk. Would *Gott* honor her Christmas wish to keep her *boppli?* Was Ethan the answer to such a wish, or had she hurt him too badly when she'd left to reverse the damage she'd done? She knew it was a long-shot, but she had to have faith that *Gott* would fulfill her Christmas wish.

Pushing herself up from the chair, Grace went back over to the stove to check on the potatoes. A sharp twinge in her abdomen sent her slowly back to the chair. It was a pain so sharp, it nearly knocked the wind out of her. She breathed slowly, closing her eyes against the pain, willing it to end. She felt the *boppli* shift position, a bump protruding from the top of her belly that could only be a wee foot. She would rest when the meal was finished, but now that the pain had subsided, she set back to work.

Minutes later, another pain assaulted her. Leaning over the counter, Grace held her breath until the pain subsided. Feeling suddenly warm, she turned on the faucet and splashed cool water over her face.

What is wrong with me? Did I bruise more than I thought when I fell?

⛧⛧⛧

Ethan finished the cradle and put it aside to let the stain dry. He patted Moo on her side before exiting the barn out into the cold. The snow had stopped for now, and he knew that meant it would not be long before the snowplows would make their way through the county. Knowing he had at least another day with Grace, he was determined more than ever to find a way to propose to her. His many trips to and from the barn had trampled enough of a path in the deep snow that he was able to get to the *haus* easier than he had even a few hours ago.

When he entered the kitchen, the smell of ham and potatoes tickled his senses. He even thought he detected the aroma of fresh-baked cornbread. His stomach rumbled at the thought of a warm meal, but more than that, he felt nervous over the chance to share it with Grace.

After removing his boots, coat, and hat, Ethan entered the kitchen and caught sight of Grace, her face flush from standing over the stove. He walked over to the sink and couldn't help but stare at her beautiful, flush face. After washing his hands, he grabbed the linen towel that hung from Grace's shoulder and wiped his hands dry. Standing so close to her, he couldn't resist scooping her rosy cheeks into his hands. He wanted to kiss her, but he feared her reaction. Grace met his gaze with expectation, giving Ethan permission to move forward.

CHAPTER 18

Greet one another with a kiss of love.
1 Peter 5:14

Grace felt the cool touch of Ethan's hands across her warm cheeks. She leaned into him, meeting his cold lips with her warm ones. Was this really happening? Or was she hallucinating from the intense pain that contracted her lower back and abdomen? Ignoring the pain, Grace deepened the kiss, wanting more from Ethan than she dared admit. If she had her way, he'd propose and her wish would be fulfilled. But she knew it wouldn't be that easy. She had no idea why Ethan was kissing her, but she didn't want him to stop. Was it possible he still loved her too?

Ethan knew he was risking a lot by kissing Grace, but he couldn't help himself. Her lips had almost lured him in, and the look in her eyes made him believe she loved him as much as he still loved her. His hands moved to the roundness of her belly.

"Grace, there's something I want to ask you," he said in-between kisses. "I want to…"

Crying out, Grace pulled away from him, the look on her face alarming. She braced herself against the counter and cried out again.

"What's wrong?" Ethan asked.

"I need to go to the hospital," Grace cried. "I think I'm in labor."

Ethan moved her slowly into the bedroom and helped her onto the bed. "I'm afraid I can't get you to the hospital. The runner on our sleigh is broken and the snowplows haven't made their way this far yet for me to be able to take the buggy."

"Call the doctor," she cried, clenching her abdomen.

Ethan was afraid to tell Grace the phones were still down when he'd checked before leaving the barn only a few minutes ago.

"How long have you been having the pains?"

Grace thought about it for a minute, panic paralyzing her. "I've been achy all day, but the strong pains have only been coming for about an hour."

"It's your first *boppli,* and labor can take eighteen hours or more. If the real pains just started an hour ago, you've got plenty of time."

Grace was suddenly irritated with him. "How do you know? You've never had a *boppli."*

"You know that *mei mamm* is a midwife, and I've taken her to the births of many *bopplies* in the community. I've heard her say the same thing to many women."

The pains assaulted Grace again with more intensity than the last one. "It's getting worse. Call the doctor. He has a sleigh."

Ethan took her hands in his and gently spoke to her. "The phones are still down, Grace. I'm sorry"

Grace began to cry and pushed his hands away. "Keep trying. I need a doctor."

Ethan pulled her shoes off and tucked her feet under the quilt. "Let's get you comfortable first. I'll go back out to the barn to check in a minute."

Bending down, he placed a soft kiss on her forehead before leaving the room. In the sitting room, he placed another split of wood on the fire and headed for the mudroom to put on his wet coat and boots to make another trip to the barn—a trip he feared would be fruitless.

ജവര

Grace prayed through the pains, begging *Gott* to make them go away. She wasn't ready to have her *boppli*—not yet. She was supposed to have it in a hospital, and the social worker was supposed to come and take the *boppli* away and give it to the adoptive parents. Was this *Gott's* way of allowing her to keep the *boppli?* But how could it be? When the snowplows came around, she would still have to relinquish the *boppli* to the social worker, but only now it would be harder if she had too much time to spend with him or her.

Up until now, Grace hadn't really thought of her *boppli* in terms of what it would be. She'd tried not to think about the reality of it during her entire pregnancy. Doctor Davis would certainly not understand her decision to give it up, and neither would Ethan. If Doctor Davis delivered the *boppli* instead her being in a hospital delivering among strangers, she would never be able to do what she knew she must do for the sake of her child.

When Ethan comes back in the haus, I will insist he call for an ambulance to take me to Elkhart General.

Gott, I'm scared. Please fix this mess I've gotten myself and my boppli into. I know I asked you to make it so I could keep my boppli as my Christmas wish, but now I'd like to change my wish. My Christmas wish is that you will take care of my boppli and give him or her the best home possible with two parents to love.

೮೦೧೪

Ethan prayed all the way from the barn to the *dawdi haus*. As he opened the door, Grace's screams rent the air. He rushed to her side not knowing what to expect. He couldn't tell her in her fragile state that the phones were still down. Not to mention, it had begun to snow again.

Despite her cries and sweat-drenched hair, Grace had never looked more beautiful to him. He wished he could marry her before the *boppli* was born to spare her the shame she must be feeling. How could he relay to her that it was her ex-husband's shame to bear and not hers? He loved her and couldn't bear that she must be feeling a mixture of emotion; he could see it in her eyes.

Grace looked at him and gritted her teeth. "I can see by the look of pity in your eyes—that you could not reach the doctor. What—am I going to do?" she asked between the contractions.

"I'm here for you, Grace," Ethan said softly.

"You can't help me," she shouted.

"I'm all you've got," Ethan said impatiently.

"No! You can't be here—when I'm giving birth," Grace cried. "You can't see me like *that*. You're not—my husband."

Ethan fumed. "Well neither is the *mann* who did this to you!"

CHAPTER 19

For everyone born of God overcomes the world.
1 John 5:4

"I have—a cell phone in my car," Grace cried. "It needs to be charged—but you can use it to call— for help."

Ethan sat on the edge of his bed and took hold of Grace's arms firmly. "I don't think you have that kind of time. As quickly as the pains are coming, you wouldn't last even if the ambulance could make it here in the deep snow. The plows haven't been out here yet. I think you're stuck with me."

Grace turned her face away. "Get—out—of— here," she said with a low growl.

"You are not getting rid of me, Grace. This might be the first birth outside of a barn I've assisted, but it can't be much different than when Moo gave birth."

Grace turned sharply. "You're comparing me—to a cow?"

Ethan tried to hide his amusement. "Of course not; this is part of nature. And there isn't any way out of it. You are in labor, and you will give birth. You can't do this by yourself, so I suggest you get used to my being here real fast."

He knew he was feeding her a harsh dose of reality, but they didn't have time for a debate. She was going to have to trust him, and he in turn would put his full trust in *Gott* to bring them through this trial in one piece. If he didn't take control of the situation, it was going to come out far worse than a little bit of embarrassment for the two of them. He meant it when he told her he wouldn't let anything happen to her, and if that meant he had to invade her privacy during the birth, then *Gott* would make it alright in the end. And though she didn't know it yet, he intended to make her his *fraa,* and that would make right the obstacles they were about to hurdle over.

"I'm going to go get some clean linens and a dishpan of clean water. When I get back, I expect you to be serious about what is best for this *boppli* that is about to make its way into this *haus—my haus.* I love you Grace, and I want you to be my *fraa.* You don't have to say anything now, but since you're already mad at me, I might as well admit I overheard you say you were divorced and thought you would have to give this *boppli* up for adoption. If I have anything to say about it, that isn't going to happen."

Ethan left the room before she could argue with him. While he readied the things for the impending birth, he tried not let fear creep into his mind at the sound of her screams from the pain. Breathing a quick prayer before returning to the room, Ethan felt confident *Gott* was answering *both* of their prayers.

ఴఙ

Grace doubled over through a strong contraction, unable to keep from letting out the cries she was trying so desperately to stifle. Had *Gott* just answered her prayer? Was her Christmas wish about to come true? Or had she imagined Ethan's proposal? She couldn't worry about that at the moment, for she was about to give birth in the presence of the only *mann* she'd ever really loved. In between the frequent contractions, Grace prayed, thanking *Gott* that she was here with Ethan at this exact time. If it hadn't happened that way, she never would have realized how much she really loved him or had the opportunity at a second chance to turn a bad situation into a *gut* one.

When Ethan returned to the room, Grace tensed a little, but she knew she had to trust him. She had lost trust over the past several months, and trusting was not going to be easy, but Ethan had never given her a reason not to trust in him. While he readied things around the room, Grace prayed in between the contractions, asking *Gott* to ease her fears.

Placing a cool cloth on Grace's forehead, Ethan tried to pray through his fears about the impending birth. He knew it was inevitable that he help her deliver the *boppli,* but he had to admit that delivering Moo's calf was a *lot* different than this was going to be. He pushed down the fears he had for Grace's and the *boppli's* safety without the presence of a doctor or a midwife. Being the son of a midwife, he had been in the vicinity of many births. He'd overheard his *mamm's* instructions enough times to remember the steps—even if he hadn't been in the room. He'd always stayed out in the kitchen keeping the husband's company. Looking back on it now, he wished he'd had the guts to assist his *mamm* the way she'd asked him to on more than one occasion.

Gott, direct my steps to deliver this boppli so that it won't bring any harm to either of these two that you have entrusted in my care. Please guard Grace's virtue during the birth and keep shame from both of us. Danki, Lord.

By the change in Grace's demeanor, Ethan knew it was time to catch the *boppli.* One final push revealed the wee one that he prayed would be his *dochder.*

CHAPTER 20

Now that you have purified yourselves by obeying the truth so that you have sincere love for your brothers, love one another deeply from the heart.
1 Peter 1:22

Grace cradled her new *dochder* in her arms, her fears and embarrassment long gone. How could she have thought she could give her *boppli* up for adoption? Even if Ethan's proposal had been only in her imagination, brought on by the stress of giving birth, she would work two jobs if need-be just to raise the new love of her life.

Ethan perched on the edge of the bed and placed a loving hand over the *boppli's* head. "What do you intend to name her?"

Grace smiled at Ethan, despite her exhaustion.

"Since she was born on Christmas Eve, I thought I would name her Noelle."

Ethan liked the sound of that. "I think Noelle Bontrager is a fine name for such a beautiful *boppli.*"

Grace looked at him with hope in her eyes. "I thought I imagined you proposing to me. You didn't do it out of pity did you?"

Ethan kissed her gently on the forehead. "Grace, I made a Christmas wish that *Gott* would bless me with a *familye* this year for Christmas. I knew it was next to impossible, but I had faith the size of a mustard seed that *Gott* would bring it to pass."

Grace smiled, tears of joy clouding her vision. "I made a Christmas wish too. I asked *Gott* to make a way for me to be able to keep my *boppli* so I wouldn't have to give her up for adoption. I'd all but lost hope until I woke up in your *haus* after I fell. I was so turned around when my car slid off the road, I had no idea I was this close to your farm. I'm so happy *Gott* brought me to you."

Ethan cradled Grace and Noelle in his arms. "I love you, Grace, and I want to marry you and raise Noelle as my own *kinner.*"

Tears streamed down Grace's cheeks. "I would like that too. I love you, Ethan, and I would love nothing more than to be your *fraa.*"

Ethan fell to his knees beside the bed, his face pointed toward heaven. "*Danki Gott. Danki* for answering our prayers and fulfilling our Christmas wishes."

ଊଓଇଆ

Ethan tucked the cradle under his arm as he braved the cold once more. Making his way to the *dawdi haus,* he couldn't help but whisper another prayer of thanks to *Gott* for bringing him a *familye.* The phones back online, he'd made arrangements for the doctor to visit at first daylight to check on Grace and the *boppli.* He'd even asked him to go by Grace's *haus* and tell her *mamm* and *daed* that she and the *boppli* were alright. Ethan found himself feeling grateful that he didn't know the phone number of her *familye* because it would have been too tempting to lecture her *daed* about Grace and Noelle and the importance of *familye.* Deep down he knew it would fall on deaf ears, and so he felt relief that Doctor Davis would be the one to deliver the news to the Fishers. Ethan prayed that they would accompany the doctor on his visit tomorrow so he could deliver the news of their impending marriage and his plans for raising Noelle.

Ethan delighted in the soft gurgles coming from his new *dochder* as he entered the room. The look in Grace's eyes made his heart swell when she set her gaze upon the cradle he'd made for Noelle. Grabbing a clean lap quilt, Ethan lined the bottom of the cradle and presented it to his betrothed.

"Is that what you were doing out in the barn all day?"

"*Jah,*" Ethan said. "I made it with a prayer in my heart that you would agree to marry me and I could raise this wee one as my own. I love you, Grace, and I couldn't be happier."

"Danki," Grace said as she leaned toward him.

Her lips touched Ethan's in a soft kiss. He cupped her face in his hands, drawing her closer and deepening the kiss.

"I love you Grace, and I promise I will take care of you and Noelle until death parts us. I suppose I should call for the Bishop first thing in the morning so he can marry us right away."

Grace suddenly felt shy at the thought of marrying Ethan, but her happiness outweighed any fear she had. She'd promised herself she'd never marry again after her marriage to Jake had been such a short-lived disaster. It was not *Gotte's wille* for her marry Jake, and she knew that now. Despite that fact that she had strayed from the righteous path, *Gott* had blessed her with a beautiful *dochder* and a second chance to put her life back on track.

Ethan left the room after kissing his betrothed one more time. She needed privacy to nurse the *boppli,* and Ethan wanted to heat up the dinner that had gone uneaten.

CHAPTER 21

Like newborn babies, crave pure spiritual milk, so that by it you may grow up in your salvation, now that you have tasted that the Lord is good.
1 Peter 2:2

Ethan jerked awake, nearly falling off the chair at the bedside of his betrothed. He'd fallen asleep in the chair after the last feeding, waiting to put Noelle back in the cradle. Grace had wanted to cuddle the *boppli* before returning her to the cradle, and Ethan found it difficult to stay awake until Grace had finished changing her new *dochder* with the make-shift diapers he had fashioned out of extra linens. Moonlight reflecting off the snow brightened the room, letting Ethan know it was still too early to be up for the day. Grace had returned Noelle to her cradle, and both were sleeping peacefully despite the chill in the air.

Stretching, Ethan worked the kinks out of his neck before rising from the chair. He moved slowly and quietly toward the front room where the fireplace needed tending. He needed to keep his new *familye* warm.

My new familye.

Ethan had to admit he liked the sound of that. But would his parents be upset with him for marrying while they were away? Under the circumstances, they couldn't expect him to wait until they were present. His parents were very supportive of him and he was confident they would accept his decision.

Tossing two logs into the fire, Ethan couldn't help but smile as he thought of being married to Grace. He'd loved her since they were in grade school together. Not only was he going to marry the woman he loved, he was a *daed*.

ৰুৎৎ

A knock at the kitchen door startled Ethan. He'd been standing at the stove waiting for the *kaffi* to be ready and daydreaming again about how happy he was. Standing on the freshly shoveled porch was Doctor Davis and Bishop Troyer. He'd forgotten about making the call. He hadn't even had time to get to the barn yet to do the milking. Between the early morning feeding and making certain the *haus* was warm enough, he'd put off his early morning duties.

There was still plenty of time to take care of everything since the sun was barely up.

"*Kume,*" Ethan said, inviting the *menner* into the small *haus.*

The fact that the Bishop had shown up without an invite made Ethan a little curious. Did he have a direct line of communication to *Gott?* How else would he have known he was needed?

After showing the doctor to the room where Grace was busy with Noelle, he offered the Bishop a cup of *kaffi.* He nodded acceptance as he took a seat at the small table in the kitchen. When Ethan sat across from him and prepared to break the news to the Bishop, he was interrupted by the look he was getting from the older *mann.*

"I had a late-night call from Abe Fisher. He wanted to make certain there wasn't anything improper with this situation with his *dochder.*"

Ethan could feel anger rising up in him over Abe's seemingly lack of care for Grace's well-being, but he kept it in check for the Bishop's sake. "I had to deliver her *boppli.*"

"Is she married to an *Englischer?*" The Bishop asked.

"He left her—divorced her."

Bishop Troyer shifted in his chair. "Is she prepared to make a confession?"

Ethan didn't want to speak for Grace; all he could do was to give his own confession. "I want to marry her. Would you marry us?"

Bishop Troyer raised an eyebrow at Ethan. "I suppose there *has* been some question of the arrangement you two have here. That would warrant an immediate marriage. Is Grace in agreement?"

Ethan's heart flip-flopped. "*Jah.*"

Doctor Davis entered the kitchen then. "Mother and baby are in perfect shape. You would have made your *mamm* proud with your midwifery services."

Bishop Troyer stood and excused himself to have a discussion with Grace in private. Ethan knew a confession was in order before they could be wed. For a moment, he wondered what she would tell him during her confession, but then he pushed down the concern for her. To him, Grace was no different than a widow. Her husband had left her against her will through no fault of her own, and the Bishop would not hold it against her. He was a fair *mann* and would treat the situation with the utmost care. Ethan sighed, eager for the Bishop to conclude his session with Grace so he could make her his *fraa.*

CHAPTER 22

For this reason a man will leave his father and mother and
be united with his wife, and the two will become one flesh.
Matthew 19:5

Grace nuzzled Ethan's neck as she slept quietly beside him. A light knock startled him out of his reverie. It had been a long day already with all the excitement of their impromptu wedding. Between the events of the past few days and the night feedings, Ethan had intended to rest beside his *fraa,* but found he couldn't sleep as peacefully as she seemed to be. He was too preoccupied with thoughts of how to break the news of his instant *familye* to his parents and too delighted that *Gott* had fulfilled *both* of their Christmas wishes.

Gently pulling his arm out from under his *fraa's* head, Ethan rose from the top of the quilt to answer the back door. He wasn't exactly in the mood for visitors, but he figured that snow would not keep Christmas guests who owned sleighs from making their rounds in the community.

A second impatient knock sounded at the back door before he reached it. A gruff looking Abe Fisher stood on the back step.

"Are you married, then?" he asked.

Ethan swallowed hard. "*Jah.*"

"*Danki* for taking care of her. I shouldn't have been so tough on her. I only hope she can forgive me," Abe confessed.

Shocked at the sudden change, Ethan could hardly be mad at Abe. If he hadn't turned her away like he had, Grace would not be here now as his *fraa.*

Abe waved a hand to *Frau Fisher* and she immediately exited the open sleigh and joined her husband on the stoop.

Ethan stepped back, allowing the older couple to enter his home. Awkwardness descended upon them, but Ethan remembered the *kaffi* he'd made and never drank just before cuddling his new *fraa* so she could get some much-needed rest while Noelle was napping.

Ethan turned to *Frau Fisher.* "Would you like to see Grace and Noelle, your new *grandkinner?*"

The woman's face lit up at the mention of the *boppli.* "She has a *dochder?*"

We have a new dochder, Ethan thought proudly.

Pointing to the room where Grace and Noelle were resting, Ethan let her walk in on her own, knowing that they probably had a lot to talk about.

ༀ∞ༀ

Grace stirred when Ethan rose from the bed they could now share. Their simple no-frills wedding had gone by faster than any traditional Amish wedding she'd ever attended. She'd assumed the Bishop had given them the shortened version to accommodate her in her weakened state. She was satisfied with the union, and was eager to get back on her feet so that she and Ethan would hopefully soon be able to seal their vows by consummating the marriage. But that would happen after the doctor's permission. For now, she would enjoy his affections in a manner fit for courting. They had their entire lives to get to know one another again and strengthen the bond of love that began in their early years.

Voices interrupted Grace's thoughts, and she was certain she'd heard her *daed.* Did her parents know she was now married to Ethan? Had her *daed* changed his mind? He'd told her a few days ago that she was not welcome until she had a husband, and she'd gotten one. *Gott* had fulfilled her Christmas wish, and Ethan's too with one action. She felt truly blessed. And now, it seemed, she was getting her *mamm* and *daed* as Christmas visitors.

Movement from the doorway caused Grace to turn her head from the frosted window. Walking toward her with a big smile on her face was her *mamm,* and in her hands was a sugar crème pie.

THE END

Please turn the page to read the complete BONUS short story,

The Christmas Prayer
(Amish Fiction)

The Christmas Prayer

Bonus short story

Chapter One

"Bartholomew Troyer, you keep your eyes on your own paper," twelve-year-old Hannah Yoder complained as she hovered over her last assignment before school let out for the Christmas holiday.

Bart was two years younger than she was, and he was always looking over at the answers she wrote during her assignments even though they weren't in the same grade. Today, however, their teacher had given the entire classroom the same assignment. No grade was exempt from answering the one question the teacher had posed. They were to write out an unselfish Christmas prayer for someone else and submit it to the teacher anonymously. Hannah didn't see the harm in writing such a bold wish for her *mamm,* but when Bart had peeked over at her paper, it had embarrassed her.

"I was just noticing you wrote the same prayer for your *mamm* that I wrote for *mei daed,"* Bart whispered. "Except I don't need a *daed* since I already have one. I asked to find him a *fraa* so I would have a *mamm.*"

"That's a selfish prayer," Hannah whispered back.

Bart scoffed at her. "You gonna tell me you aren't asking for your *mamm* to find a husband so you can have a new *daed?"*

Hannah pursed her lips. "I didn't say that," she admitted. "It's more important that *mei mamm* gets married again so she doesn't have to work so hard to take care of me on her own."

The teacher clapped her hands together and reprimanded the two of them for talking. Hannah shot Bart a dirty look before turning her paper over. She turned her head and looked out the window into the school yard where snow fluttered around lazily. She couldn't wait to be dismissed for the day so she would have some free time to enjoy the snow. She was always so busy with chores that by the time Saturday came every week, she didn't have the energy to play. Between school and chores, Hannah felt the stress of being the only child of a widow.

Hannah's *daed* had died from pneumonia when she was only three years old, so she barely knew him, but that didn't make her miss him any less. Since they'd moved to the community at the beginning of the school year, she'd heard that Bart was the son of a widower. Her *mamm* didn't seem interested in remarrying so she'd never mentioned it to her.

Bart's *daed* was the only widower in the community, and although Hannah found Bart to be an annoying tag-along, she would accept the idea of the two of them becoming *familye* if it meant her *mamm* didn't have to work so hard. And perhaps if Bart now had the same prayer, it might mean a better chance of being answered. She hoped having a husband would make her *mamm* happy like the other *mamms* in the community. She shied away from social gatherings, claiming the other women didn't understand her situation, but Hannah was old enough to know her *mamm* didn't like all the chatter about their husbands.

Hannah's daydreams came to a sudden halt when the teacher rang the school bell; school was officially suspended until after the new-year. Placing her assignment on the teacher's desk before entering the coat room, Hannah reflected on how she wanted to spend her vacation from school.

All the students crowded the back of the room and talked loudly while they excitedly put their coats, hats and mittens on. Hannah wrapped her homemade scarf around her neck and ducked out into the wind that was slowly picking up. The snow thickened, swirling around them as the other students fanned out into different directions toward their homes. Hannah was grateful the walk back to her cousin's *haus* where she and her *mamm* resided was not far.

Bart ran up alongside her to catch up to her.

"Wait," he called behind her. "I want to talk to you about your Christmas prayer."

Hannah turned around sharply. "There's nothing to talk about."

Bart looked up at her sheepishly. "M-maybe we can help each other."

Scoffing and raising an eyebrow, Hannah picked up her pace in the cold. "How can *you* help *me?*"

Bart did a run-walk to keep up with Hannah who had always been a fast walker. "We can figure out a way to get your *mamm* together with my *daed.*"

"That sounds a lot like putting our noses in adult business. Wouldn't your *daed* have a *talk* with you out in the barn if he knew you were getting into his business?"

"*Nee,*" he fibbed. "I think he would be so happy to have a *fraa* he would forget all about any mischief I'd gotten into."

"I think you are asking for trouble," Hannah said. "Besides, we're young; what can we do?"

Bart smiled at her mischievously. "I will think of a plan and let you know tomorrow. Can I come over in the afternoon?"

Hannah was getting annoyed with Bart. "*Nee.* I have chores—too many to play your silly games that will never work."

Bart stood in front of Hannah, causing her to stop suddenly in her tracks. "I'll help you with your chores if you'll help me. I want *mei daed* to have a *fraa* for Christmas."

Hannah knew getting their parents to know each other, fall in love, and marry was not going to happen before Christmas, but she was more than happy to let Bart help with her chores. Opportunities like this one didn't come along that often, and she was prepared to take full advantage of the help.

Chapter Two

Myra Yoder wiped her hands on the linen towel as she moved away from the stove to answer the door. Who would visit this early in the morning, and why would anyone knock at the *dawdi haus* instead of the main *haus?* Certainly her *dochder,* Hannah, would not knock on the door, so who could it be?

Opening the door, Myra was assaulted by a sharp wind and snowflakes stinging her cheeks.

That's strange. There's no one here. Am I hearing things?

Hannah had trampled the snow enough near the porch that there was no deciphering if there were fresh footprints. Puzzled, Myra closed the door and set back to work making Hannah's breakfast so she would have something warm to eat when she finished feeding the animals in the barn. Myra's *bruder* would send Hannah in with a fresh pail of milk from the morning milking, and it would make a nice hot cup of cocoa for the little girl who would be frozen to the bone by the time she returned to the tiny *haus* they resided in.

Myra had moved to be near her husband's *familye* when she had gotten married so many years ago. But after her beloved died, she couldn't bear to leave the home they had made together, even though it had been for only five short years. When she could no longer keep up the home on her own, she had reluctantly moved back to Shipshewana to live in the *dawdi haus* on her *bruder's* land. It was nice to be back with *familye* again, but it wasn't the same as having her own *familye.*

A sudden knock at the back door pulled Myra from her reverie. She was tempted to forget the door, but on the chance that Hannah was too cold to turn the knob, she went to see who it was. Once again, no one was there, but this time, she found a beautifully woven basket at her feet. She picked it up, inhaling the aroma of a single, scented pinecone at the bottom of the basket. Cinnamon and nutmeg tickled her senses as she wondered who could have left such a gift. Despite the wind, she stepped out onto the porch and looked around for the gift-giver, but found no one.

Smiling, Myra took her gift inside the small kitchen and set it in the center of the table. Was Hannah surprising her with an early Christmas gift? If so, where would she have gotten such a beautifully hand-made basket? Such an item would have cost money they didn't have. Trying not worry, Myra decided she would enjoy the gift.

She knew her *dochder* was a sensible girl and would never spend money they couldn't spare. Surely she would have worked off the debt in some way— perhaps cleaning the blackboard after school for the teacher, or some extra chore for her *bruder* or his *fraa*. She'd been entertaining her young cousins quite a bit lately, so perhaps her *onkel* had given her a small reward for her hard work in watching his *kinner*. Myra felt guilty at times for all the hard work her *dochder* did, but never once did the child complain. She was always happy and cheerful, and that brought blessings to Myra's heart.

Pulling the pan of bacon out of the oven, Myra placed it on a plate and covered it with another plate to keep it warm. Pumpkin muffins waited on the table in a small bowl with a linen towel over them to keep in the warmth, while Myra dished out the scrambled eggs onto clean plates. Just before she poured the juice into glasses, Hannah came stomping into the kitchen, trying to clear the snow from her boots.

Standing in a puddle of melted snow, Hannah gave her *mamm* the pail of fresh milk and then set her gaze upon the table and the basket in the center.

"Where did that come from?" she asked.

Myra looked startled. "You mean it's not from you?"

"*Nee,* it's much too beautiful for me to have made. And it smells *wunderbaar.*"

"Indeed it does," Myra agreed.

Hannah pulled off her knitted hat, her hair sticking up from the static. "Where do you suppose it came from?" she asked as she smoothed her flyaway hair.

"I heard a knock at the door, but whoever left it didn't stick around long enough to wait for me to answer."

Hannah's eyes grew wide. "You mean it was left here by someone we don't know?"

Myra finished setting the table for breakfast. "It looks that way."

Hannah sat down and waited for her *mamm* despite her growling stomach. "Why would someone do such a thing?"

"The same thing happened to *mei* cousin, and it turned out to be from a suitor."

Hannah immediately thought about her Christmas prayer. Was it possible her prayer was already being answered? Then her thoughts turned to Bart. Had he come up with a plan and decided to execute it on his own? He was too immature to think of such an elaborate plan—wasn't he? Even if he had, where would he have gotten the money to afford such an extravagant gift? There were many basket makers in Nappanee where they'd moved from, but she wasn't aware of any in this community. They hadn't been here long enough for her to know each member's contribution to the community. But she knew her *onkel* and *aenti* would know. If Bart was in some way responsible for the gift, Hannah didn't want her *mamm* getting hurt by such a scheme.

"Maybe you should ask *onkel* who makes baskets in the community," Hannah said.

"*Jah,*" she said. If it was a potential suitor, Myra wasn't certain she was ready for such a thing—was she?

Chapter Three

"Hurry, Hannah," Myra called to her *dochder* from the kitchen. "Your *onkel* is waiting."

Myra opened the back door and found another pinecone on the top rail of the porch resting in the snow. She picked it up with her mitten-clad hand and brought it to her nose. She breathed in the sweet smell of warm cinnamon and nutmeg, and wondered how she could be so lucky to have a gift two days in a row. But how was it that the giver had gone unnoticed each morning? Myra walked out toward the barn where her *bruder's familye* waited for them in the sleigh. Henry assisted her into the back of the sleigh with his *fraa*, Susanna, and their *boppli*.

"Where did you get that pinecone?" Susanna asked.

Myra held it up so her *schweschder*-in-law could smell it. "Yesterday I heard a knock at the door and there was a basket on the step with one of these scented pinecones in it. Now this morning, I find another pinecone, but I have no idea how they got there."

"What kind of basket?" Henry asked over his shoulder.

Myra tucked the pinecone into the pocket of her coat. "It was handmade, and very intricately woven. Whoever made it is very talented at his craft."

Hannah ran up to the sleigh and sat up front with her *onkel* and her cousin.

"That sounds like the work of Jeb Troyer. Do you know him?" Henry asked.

"*Nee,*" Myra said. "Not that I know of. I've only been to a few Sunday services here, so I don't remember who I've met for sure and for certain. Why would he give me the gifts without introducing himself?"

Henry jiggled the reins, setting the horses in motion. "He's a single *mann*—a widower. Maybe he is getting ready to invite you for a sleigh ride."

Myra felt her heart flutter. She wasn't ready for that. Why would he be giving her gifts when she didn't even know him? Had she met him at Church and forgotten? If she'd forgotten, he must not have made a memorable impression on her.

"How exciting for you," Susanna said.

Myra gulped down fear. "I'm certain there must be another explanation."

Henry turned his face to the side and talked over his shoulder as he kept his eye on the path in front of the sleigh. "You will get the chance to find out soon enough. The services are at Jeb's *haus* this week."

Fear encapsulated Myra like warmth from a window on a sunny, winter day. She would never approach a *mann* she didn't know to ask if he sent her a gift—especially not a widower. Her older *bruder* had talked to her when she'd first arrived back in Shipshewana, telling her she was still too young to remain a widow, lecturing her on the importance of getting married again. At first, she'd taken it as his way of saying he didn't want to shoulder the burden of her and Hannah, but then he'd voiced his concerns over her happiness and that of Hannah. Myra felt guilty almost on a daily basis for not being able to give Hannah a new *daed,* but she also knew it would be in *Gott's* timing. After all, she and Hannah had only been here for a few months, and the opportunity hadn't yet presented itself.

Had it now?

Henry steered the sleigh down the lane toward a fair-sized farm where it seemed the entire community had arrived before they had. If Jeb lived this close to them, it was entirely possible for him to have left the basket and pinecones without too much trouble. He could have slipped through the dense woods that separated their farms without ever being noticed. Henry steered the sleigh near the rest of the buggies and sleighs. He and Hannah hopped out, and then Henry gave assistance to Myra and Susanna.

Feeling her knees buckle as her feet hit the soggy ground, Myra wasn't certain she had the nerve to walk into the home of the unknown *mann* who may or may not have left her the gifts. Susanna saw her hesitation and tucked her free hand in the crook of Myra's elbow.

"Kume," Susanna whispered. "It will be alright. The *mann* isn't going to bite you. He's a *gut mann,* you'll see."

That's exactly what Myra was afraid of. If he was too nice, she would have a tough time turning him down. She certainly didn't like being in a position where she could hurt his feelings by rejecting him. But she had to—didn't she?

Chapter Four

Hannah couldn't wait for the Sunday service to end. She'd overheard her *mamm* talking about getting a new pinecone on the way to the service and knew she had to talk to Bart first thing. She fidgeted, and her three-year-old cousin, Anna, looked up at her. She smiled at Anna, knowing if she didn't sit still, her *mamm* would reprimand her at the conclusion of the service—especially if she provoked little Anna to imitate her restless behavior.

Replacing the *Ausbund* on the bench seat next to her after they finished singing the hymn, Hannah raced to the back door of Bart's *haus* and put her coat and mittens on, waiting for him to join her. It wasn't long before Bart noticed Hannah, put on his own coat, and tugged her out the back door. Out in the yard,

Hannah stopped in the bank of snow that had been shoveled aside for visitors to have a clear pathway to the *haus.*

"Are you the one who put that basket and pinecones on our back step yesterday and then again this morning?"

Bart flashed a sheepish look. "Maybe. What if I did?"

Hannah's lips formed an angry line. "Don't play games with me, Bart. If you did it, tell me then."

Bart rolled his eyes. "I did it. So what? You gonna tell on me?"

Hannah thought about it for a minute.

Bart stepped forward, closing the space between them. "Well, are you?"

Hannah stepped back defensively. "Of course not. But I don't want *mei mamm* getting hurt over this scheme of yours. What is going to happen when your *daed* finds out you've done this? Parents *always* find out what we do wrong."

Bart kicked at the snow bank, sending clumps of snow onto the freshly shoveled path. "I haven't thought that far ahead. I guess I should stop giving her the pinecones before it gets out of control."

Hannah glared at him. "It's already out of control. You didn't see the look of happiness on *mei mamm's* face when she talked about the gift—a gift that she thinks is from your *daed,* when it's really from *you!"*

"*Mei daed* made it, so it kind of makes it from him." Bart said in his defense.

Hannah poked Bart in the arm. "You are the one who left it on our doorstep—not your *daed.*"

Bart lowered his gaze. "I should have thought this through a little more before I acted. What can I do now? I can't take it back."

Hannah paced, trampling down the snow. "Maybe we can give this a push in the right direction. You already started this, so we can't turn back now. Christmas is only a little more than a week away. If we want this to work, we have to work a little faster. I can suggest we make some of *mei mamm's* gingerbread cookies. Then I will give some to you to take back to your *haus,* and you can give them to your *daed.*"

Bart placed his hands on his hips. "If I do that, he's gonna ask me where I got them. What do I tell him?"

"Tell him the truth—well, that they're from *mei mamm*—that she baked them."

"That doesn't sound much like the truth," Bart complained.

Hannah pursed her lips. "It's no more the truth than you leaving pinecones on our porch."

Bart kicked at the snow again. "Why do I get the feeling I'm gonna be in trouble for Christmas?"

Hannah sighed. "We both will if this doesn't work."

ଡ଼ଔଔ

"What do you suppose the two of them have been talking about all this time?" Henry asked Susanna as he peeked over his *fraa's* shoulder out the window at Hannah and Bart.

"Isn't that Jeb Troyer's *buwe?*" she asked.

"Jah, and it looks like they are in the middle of a very serious discussion."

"More like a dispute," Susanna said.

Henry chuckled. "Do you suppose those two are responsible for the basket and pinecone gifts Myra has gotten?"

"They're too young to be playing match-maker, aren't they?"

"Nee, they're plenty old enough to team up so each of them gets the parent they're missing. I'd say that's what this is about if I had to guess."

"I hope this doesn't end badly for your *schweschder,"* Susanna said with worry in her tone.

Myra came up behind Susanna. "Would you like me to hold the *boppli* so you can eat?"

"Danki, Myra. I am very hungry this afternoon."

Susanna handed over the *boppli* to Myra and went toward the kitchen where the food waited along the counters. The Elders were already seated with their plates, as were most of the *menner* and the *kinner.* Bart and Hannah came in from outside, stomping the snow from their boots.

"Kume, Hannah," Susanna said. "Get some of this food while it's still hot. It'll warm you up."

Bart and Hannah each grabbed a plate and piled it high with meat and potato dishes, as well as warm bread rolls. Hannah had wanted to avoid her *mamm* for now, so she sat with Susanna, while Bart went into another room in the *haus* to sit with his *daed* and the rest of the *menner*.

When they were seated, Susanna turned to Hannah discretely and spoke quietly below the level of chatter among the women in the room. "I see you made a new friend."

Hannah looked at her quizzically.

"The Troyer *buwe,*" Susanna said. "Do you know him from school?"

"*Jah,* he's kind of annoying," Hannah whispered.

"It looked like the two of you were having quite the discussion outside."

Hannah's expression fell. "Did *mei mamm* see me out there talking to him?"

"*Nee,*" her *aenti* said. "Are the two of you up to something?"

"We were talking about a school assignment," Hannah said nervously. It wasn't a lie.

Susanna smiled knowingly. "School is out for winter break. What kind of an assignment would the two of you be working on over Christmas break?"

Hannah smiled. "It's a surprise!"

Chapter Five

Myra tried to keep her mind on the wash she was hanging on the line. She needed to hurry before her fingers became icicles, but her mind kept drifting to the pinecone that was tucked away in her apron pocket. Had the handsome Jeb Troyer really been the giver of such a gift? Susanna had pointed him out as the basket-maker in the community and the host of the service yesterday. She hadn't talked to him, but they had made eye-contact briefly before Myra had turned away shyly.

From there, she had sneaked a few glances at him from across the room, and every time she tried to steal a glance, he turned his gaze upon her as though he somehow knew she was looking at him. It terrified and excited her at the same time, but she eventually gave up all attempts out of embarrassment. At one time, she had been close enough to see the green in his hazel eyes.

Those piercing eyes...

Hannah smacked the linens with a stick to knock the ice from them. The noise startled Myra, and she chided herself for thinking romantic thoughts of a *mann* when she was supposed to be doing her chores. Guilt crept into her heart for thinking about Jeb Troyer in the same manner a woman would think of a *mann* she was attracted to. Was she attracted to him? She couldn't answer that question honestly to herself without feeling even more guilt. What would Hannah think if she knew her *mamm* was thinking about a *mann* that wasn't her husband? Was it fair for her to remain a widow for the rest of her days on this earth?

"I can finish if you're too cold," Hannah called from the other end of the clothesline.

"*Nee,* this is the last one," Myra called back. "Let's go inside and make some hot cocoa."

After smacking the last bed sheet to remove the ice, Hannah followed her *mamm* inside the *dawdi haus* to warm up. After removing her coat, Myra placed the pinecone into the basket in the center of the table.

Hannah looked at her wide-eyed. "You got another one?"

Myra nodded, trying to control the smile that spread across her lips.

Gulping down shame for tricking her *mamm,* Hannah pulled off her wet mittens and stuffed them on the pegs near the door so they would dry before she had to go back out again. They'd hung the last load of laundry for the week, and though Hannah felt like they'd accomplished much already, she felt suddenly down. Had she done the right thing in telling Bart they would continue with the charade? Noting the whimsical look on her *mamm's* face as she poured milk into the saucepan for hot cocoa left her wondering.

ဆဂ

Jeb Troyer looked high and low for the newest basket he'd made. It was a new style he had experimented on, and he thought he'd left it on the shelf above his work bench in the barn. Was he so distracted by thoughts of Myra Yoder this morning, that he couldn't remember a simple thing like where he'd put his new basket?

Jeb had even counted out the number of pinecones he needed to fill his orders, and he seemed to be missing three. Had he miscounted, or did he need to make another batch? Feeling a little frustrated over having to make a new batch just to fill one order, Jeb set to work mixing oils and spices in his small workspace in the corner of the barn. This was his busiest time of the year since the added cinnamon-scented pinecones brought in extra income above his basket weaving. He was thankful for the dense acre of pine trees that separated his property from Henry's.

Thinking of Myra being in such close proximity to him brought heat to his face. They'd made eye contact several times at the service yesterday before she shyly turned her gaze from him, only to grace him with it once more before she left with her *bruder's familye*. Her blue eyes had mesmerized him, and the way her wavy brown hair continuously fell loose from her *kapp* had made him think how much he desired to run his fingers through the silky tresses. He'd been a widow since Bart's *mamm* had died during the birth of their second child. The doctor hadn't been able to save either of them, leaving Jeb alone to raise two-year-old Bart without her.

Is it wrong for me to be interested in a woman who is not my fraa? Gott, ease my conscience about being a widower. Let your will be done.

Bart stormed into the barn just then, wind and snow blowing in with him. He stomped his feet. "It's pretty cold today."

"Have you seen the new basket I finished a few days ago? I was trying out a new style, but I can't find the example I made."

Bart shrugged. "They all look the same to me, *Daed.*"

It wasn't a lie; so why did it feel so much like a lie? Out of all the baskets on his *daed's* shelf, why did he have to take the one he would miss? He'd chosen it because of its uniqueness, but he had no idea it was the only one of its kind.

He'd never had an interest in the basket weaving, but he loved collecting the pinecones with his *daed*. It was one of the few *fun* things they did anymore. It seemed like every year he grew older, the more chores were piled on him. His least favorite was helping with the laundry. To Bart, that was the work that a *mamm* should do—same for cooking.

"How would you like to go out and gather another batch of pinecones for me?" Jeb asked his son.

Bart tipped his head to the side. "You want me to go by myself?"

Jeb nodded without looking up from his work. Feeling disappointed, Bart sighed as he ventured out into the snowy day without his *daed*.

Chapter Six

When Hannah came in from the barn with a fresh pail of milk from the morning milking, her *mamm* was at the table preparing what looked to be gingerbread cookies. A breakfast consisting of egg bread and bacon sat on the counter waiting for Hannah to return from her morning chores.

Myra looked up with a smile. "I thought we could make gingerbread cookies today."

Hannah smiled. This was going to be easier than she thought. "I was thinking the same thing."

"I was also hoping we could make enough to share," her *mamm* said.

"With who?" Hannah asked curiously.

"We only have one close neighbor, and we haven't made an effort to reach out to them since we've been here," Myra said pointing toward Jeb's farm.

Hannah pointed the same direction. "You mean Bart Troyer and his *daed?*"

Myra smiled. "You must know him from school, *jah?*"

Hannah nodded, her brows pinching together. Was her *mamm* aware of who had given her the gifts, or was she finally deciding that the idea of being a permanent widow, as *Onkel* had referred to her, was something she needed to work on changing? Either way, her *mamm* was playing right into the prayers she and Bart had prayed, and this would make the plan work sooner if her *mamm* cooperated—even if unknowingly.

"*Jah,* I think that's a *gut* idea. I will be happy to take them over for you when we finish," Hannah offered.

"*Danki,*" her *mamm* said with a smile.

Myra put a tea-towel over the batter and set it on the counter so they could have some breakfast before it got cold.

ഇൽ

Jeb heard a light knock on the front door just as he finished adding another log to the fire. When he opened it, a younger version of Myra Yoder stood on the porch, a plastic container in her hands.

She held out the closed container toward him with a smile. "I brought you some gingerbread cookies. *Mei mamm* made them, and I helped her. "

Jeb bent forward and accepted the container of cookies from the eager little girl. "Who is your *mamm*—so I know who to thank?"

"I'm Hannah Yoder, and *mei mamm* is Myra."

Bart came up beside his *daed.* "What are you doing here, Hannah?"

"I brought gingerbread cookies for your *daed.* They're from *mei mamm.* "

Jeb looked back and forth between the two, wondering if the smiles on their faces meant they were up to something, but he would play along if it meant fresh cookies were in store for them.

"Please come in and join us. We have fresh milk," Jeb offered.

"*Nee, *" Hannah said, eyeing Bart. "I must go home. *Mei mamm* needs me to help with chores."

Jeb thanked her for the cookies and went into the kitchen to make hot cocoa for his son. Bart followed him and sat at the table in the kitchen. He opened the container; the warm aroma of gingerbread permeated the room. It warmed Jeb's heart to think of Myra blessing him with such a gift. He sat down with his son and bit into one of the cookies. Warm ginger filled his mouth, and the thought behind them warmed his heart. It felt *gut* to hope again.

჻ஐ

Hannah struggled with guilt as she walked home from the Troyer's farm. After seeing the hope in the eyes of Bart's *daed*, Hannah wondered if she had done the right thing. She could have just as easily told the *mann* that they were extra cookies; she didn't have to tell him the cookies were from her *mamm*. Because of the gifts, two people were now filled with hope for something that may never happen, and it was all her fault. She couldn't even blame Bart; he was younger than she was, and though he was smart, what they had done was not smart. They should have left it alone after writing the prayer, but now they had taken things into their own hands instead of trusting *Gott*.

Hannah knew that works were important, but only if they matched up with *Gott's* plan for their lives. Had everything fallen into place because *Gott* was working a miracle in their lives, or were she and Bart pushing their own agenda? Either way, they were in too deep to turn back now. If this didn't work, they would have to find a way to fix it to be certain no one was hurt. Hannah felt sad at the possibility of causing hurt to her *mamm's* heart. Though she didn't remember her *daed,* her *mamm* had spent a lot of time being sad. But now, she was happier than Hannah had ever seen her. It was too much responsibility to hold her *mamm's* happiness in her hands.

Gott, please help me so I don't hurt mei mamm because of my dishonest actions. Bless Bart's daed too. Forgive me and Bart for being selfish with our parents, but we want them to be happy. Please don't let either of them lose the happiness they have now.

Hannah walked into the kitchen of her *onkel's dawdi haus* to find her *mamm* kneading bread dough. She had dawdled too much on the walk home, and she was too late to help, but her *mamm* didn't reprimand her. She seemed in a better mood than she'd ever seen her. Was it possible that even the thought of having a new love was *gut* for her *mamm?* Hannah suddenly felt at ease with what she had done. She wasn't certain if it was because *Gott* had forgiven her, or if He was allowing her the opportunity to bring true happiness to her *mamm*. It felt *gut* to see her *mamm* with a constant smile on her face. It put a smile in Hannah's heart, and for the first time in a long time, it felt *gut* to be happy because her *mamm* was happy.

Chapter Seven

Myra sighed pure delight when she opened the back door to find another scented pinecone on the porch rail. She breathed in the cold air and watched the snowflakes for a few minutes before returning to the warmth of the *dawdi haus.* It was nearly Christmas, and she was getting the most exciting gift she had gotten in too many years to count. But what was Jeb waiting for? Why was he being so secretive? She enjoyed the intrigue, especially since she was still getting used to the idea. Perhaps he, too, was getting used to the idea. Myra was in no hurry to move things along. She'd been a widow for over nine years; what was a few more days or weeks or months? So far, though, she admittedly liked the idea.

Another knock came at the door, causing Myra's heart to skip a beat. Was Jeb back to invite her on a sleigh ride like her *bruder* said he would? Myra opened the door with a shaky hand, only to breathe relief when she saw it was her *schweschder*-in-law.

"Susanna, *kume,*" she said. "It's too cold for the *boppli.* Why didn't you just let yourself in?"

Susanna pushed the *boppli* into Myra's arms as she ambled her way into the *haus.* "My hands were too full, so I used my foot to knock on the door."

Susanna set containers of food down on Myra's table. "This is the food we have to make for dinner tonight at *mei* cousin, Jeb's *haus.*"

Myra's face drained of all color. "You didn't tell me *Jeb* was your cousin when you invited me to your *familye* dinner last week! You asked if I wanted to go with you to have a meal with your *familye.*"

Susanna shrugged sheepishly. "Did I forget to mention that Jeb was my cousin? Well, no matter. We have to make the bread and desert, and we have all these potatoes to peel and shred for the sour cream and chive potato casserole. We might as well get to work because I already told Jeb you were coming, so you can't back out of it."

Susanna had a knack for talking very fast—so fast that others could not get in a word to stop her once she got started. Myra knew it was useless to try to talk her way out of attending the meal, so she handed the *boppli* over to Hannah so she and Susanna could get to work to preparing for the meal.

೮೦೦೪

Jeb buttoned up his best royal blue shirt and looped his arms through his suspenders. Running his hand across the stubble on his angled jaw, he wondered if he had time to shave again. Looking at the clock on the bureau, he decided against it. If he shaved when he was in a hurry, there was more chance he would cut himself, and he felt he would look better with a little scruff on his face than red marks from shaving.

Bart stood at the doorway of his *daed's* room watching him. He hadn't remembered seeing his *daed* look happier than he had over the past few days. Was it possible that his and Hannah's prayers were being answered as quickly as they'd hoped?

A knock at the door interrupted both father and son. Their guests were here, and Bart hoped it was the two that might possibly be his new *familye* soon.

Jeb felt his heart thump against his ribcage as he helped Myra out of her coat. She was shy, but accommodating. He even thought he'd heard her whisper a very quiet *"Danki"* before he hung it up on the pegs near the door. He took Susanna's and Henry's coats as well, while Hannah opted to leave hers on after Bart asked her to play in the snow for a few minutes before the table was set.

The *menner* stayed in the front room while Susanna and Myra joined Jeb's *schweschder* and *mudder* in the kitchen. Jeb sat in a chair opposite his *daed* so he could have a better view of the women in the kitchen. He watched as Myra made herself at home in his kitchen and talked freely with his *familye.* His mind wandered, picturing Myra alone in the kitchen preparing meals for him and Bart. She looked naturally *at home* in his *haus,* and he found himself wondering what it would be like to have her with him permanently—as his *fraa.*

Soon, the women had set the table and had summoned everyone to eat. Conveniently, everyone left the seat open to Jeb's right for Myra. Taking his place at the head of the large table, Jeb bowed his head for the silent prayer before the meal. He included Myra in that prayer, hoping *Gott* would not find it selfish of him to ask for the possibility of a new *fraa* for him and a new *mamm* for Bartholomew.

Myra sat nervously close to Jeb at the crowded table. She tried to interject here and there during conversations, but mostly found herself pushing the food around her plate. It wasn't that she didn't like the food; Susanna's potato recipe was one of her favorites. Being so near to Jeb had made her feel a little self-conscious.

At the conclusion of the meal, Myra rose from her chair as Jeb held the back of it for her. He was a gentle *mann,* and Myra admired that. During the meal she had overheard some of the conversation between the *menner,* and it was also obvious that he had a sense of humor—another quality she revered.

The kitchen was abuzz with women cleaning and clanging dishes to make way for desert. Susanna cut a slice of pie and pushed it into Myra's hands.

"Go give this to Jeb, will you? You haven't talked to him all evening."

Myra stood there with the plate of pie. "I can't give this to him; he'll think I'm interested in him!"

Susanna smiled. "You know that was the whole point of this dinner tonight, don't you?"

Myra looked around the kitchen at the new faces whose eyes all set upon her. "You were all in on this?"

They all nodded. "We thought you knew," said Jeb's *schweschder*.

Myra could feel her cheeks warming, wondering if Jeb had been in on the scheme as well.

Chapter Eight

Myra stood bravely in front of Jeb with the slice of pie, trying to keep the fork from rattling from the unsteadiness of her hand. Jeb stood to receive the dish from her.

"If this pie is half as tasty as the cookies you sent over here yesterday, I'm sure I'll enjoy it," he said with a smile that brought heat to Myra's face.

"Susanna made the pie, but I helped her peel the apples." Myra felt stupid for saying such a thing, but she didn't know what else to say.

She looked into Jeb's hazel eyes, noting the kindness there. She was falling for him, despite every effort to guard her heart. His smile warmed her, making her forget the rest of the world existed.

"*Danki* for the cookies. We polished off the last of them this afternoon."

Myra blushed at his appreciation. "It was the least I could do for you after you went to so much trouble to leave the hand-woven basket and the scented pinecones on my doorstep every day."

Jeb put the pie plate down on the table and looked at her with confusion. "I didn't leave anything on your doorstep."

Myra felt the blood draining from her face while her heart did somersaults behind her ribcage. Excusing herself abruptly, Myra swallowed down tears as she ran to the back door for her coat.

Susanna was at her side as she pushed her arms into her coat sleeves. "Please bring Hannah home with you," Myra said with a shaky voice. "I have to go. I suddenly don't feel well."

Susanna instinctively put a hand to Myra's forehead even though she didn't think she was physically ill. She pulled Myra into a quick hug before she pushed her away to run out the door.

Myra walked swiftly, her feet crunching the new snow beneath every hasty step toward a home she felt suddenly lost in. She didn't belong here. Who was she kidding? A *mann* as handsome as Jeb would never be interested in her. The look on his face when she mentioned the basket and the pinecones said it all. The gifts were not from him, and she had never felt more humiliated.

৪০৫৪

Susanna smacked her cousin in the arm. "What did you say to Myra that made her run off?"

Jeb's eyes grew wide. "I didn't mean to upset her. She thanked me for leaving her a basket and scented pinecones on her doorstep, but when I told her I didn't do it, she didn't give me a chance to explain."

Crossing her arms over her ample bosom, Susanna gave him a look of disapproval he hadn't seen from her since they were young. "What is your explanation?"

He held his hands up defensively. "I don't have one! I didn't leave them on her doorstep," he admitted sadly. "But I *was* missing a newly woven basket and a few pinecones this week."

"Henry and I saw Hannah and Bart talking after Sunday service," Susanna said. "Do you suppose they had a hand in this?"

Jeb called his son and Hannah into the room. They both stood at attention, guilt invading their expressions.

"Did the two of you have anything to do with the basket and pinecones left on Hannah's doorstep for her *mamm*?"

"It was my fault," Bart bravely spoke up.

"I knew about it," Hannah admitted with downcast eyes.

Jeb's look softened. "Why would the two of you do such a thing?" He turned to Hannah then. "Your *mamm* thought that I left them. When she found out I didn't leave them for her, she got very upset and went home."

Bart lowered his head. "If it wasn't for that prayer, we wouldn't be in this mess."

"What prayer?" Jeb asked.

"The one our teacher had us write on the last day of school. When I looked over at Hannah's paper and saw that she had the same prayer, I thought it was an answer from *Gott*. I thought that if we could get you together with Hannah's *mamm* then you wouldn't be lonely anymore."

"I know your heart was in the right place, Bart, but those things should be left up to *Gott* and the grownups." Jeb pulled his son into a hug.

Turning to Hannah, Jeb smiled. "Is that why you brought those cookies here yesterday?"

Hannah shook her head. "*Nee,* that was *mei mamm's* idea. She wanted to do something nice for you."

Jeb felt his heart flutter.

She liked him after all.

"You should probably explain all of this to your *mamm* when you get home," he said to Hannah.

Hannah felt more guilty than ever. She'd managed to hurt her *mamm* despite the fact she didn't want to. What started out as an opportunity to help her *mamm* had turned into an opportunity for heartache. She would have to make her *mamm* understand that she only meant to help, and she would apologize.

Jeb bid his *familye* farewell one-by-one. It had been quite an exciting evening. He thought of Myra and how hurt she'd looked. It made him feel bad since he felt he already cared about her a little bit. More than that, he was interested in getting to know her better, and he worried the misunderstanding between them would hurt their chances for pursuing more than friendship. He hadn't thought he was ready to make a move in that direction, but now that he'd met her and spoken to her, he was definitely ready.

And then it dawned on him; he knew exactly what he needed to do.

Chapter Nine

A knock at the back door startled Myra. She set down the spoon that stirred the bubbling oatmeal and turned off the burner. She was not in the mood this morning for more humiliation. She'd spent too much time last night second-guessing her decision to pursue the possibility of a relationship with Jeb.

Myra wiped her hands on the linen towel and opened the door, shocked at what she saw.

Jeb stood on the back stoop, pinecone in hand, a smile on his face. "The others might not have been from me, but this one is." Jeb held out the pinecone and placed it in Myra's hand, allowing his fingers to linger over hers.

Myra pulled her hand away; she didn't want his pity. Startled, Jeb tried not to react to her sudden change in demeanor.

Jeb cleared his throat to cover his nervousness.

"May I have the pleasure of your company on a sleigh ride this evening?" he asked.

Myra looked beyond Jeb at Hannah who stood in the yard bobbing her head up and down furiously. Her eyes were wide and the smile on her face warmed Myra's heart. It was a chance for her *dochder* to redeem herself after the sorrow she felt over the mishap. Myra certainly couldn't disappoint Hannah, who had the hope of making her *mamm* happy through her Christmas prayer. It was painfully obvious Hannah was eager for her to go.

After leaving Jeb's *haus* last night, Hannah had come to her and confessed her involvement in the mix-up over the pinecones. The girl was so distraught over the possibility of making her *mamm* so unhappy that she'd cried for some time before Myra was able to calm her down. Now, she stood behind Jeb, knee-deep in the snow practically begging her to take Jeb's offer. How could she disappoint her *dochder?* Myra would have to put aside her own worries that Jeb might be offering out of pity. She prayed not, but only time would tell.

"*Jah,*" Myra relented.

The smile that spread across Jeb's face made Myra wonder if she'd been wrong about him.

ହଢ

Jeb showed up promptly at seven o'clock. Myra had worn her thickest stockings, and had even readied an extra lap-quilt in case what Jeb had in his sleigh wouldn't be enough. It was a crisp, clear night—perfect for a romantic sleigh ride under the stars. But was she putting too much hope in this gesture on Jeb's part? She had prayed most of the afternoon that *Gott* would guard her heart from falling for a *mann* who might not be interested in her.

Jeb took her mitten-clad hand in his and assisted her into the sleigh. Even through the heavy, knitted mittens she could feel the warmth of his hand. Jeb settled in close beside her and covered them with the lap-quilts. Picking up the reins, Jeb set the horses in motion, the bells on their necks chiming in rhythm with the clip-clop of their feet against the packed snow on the trail.

Once they cleared the canopy of snow-covered trees, stars ignited the indigo sky, and the moon's glow illuminated the blanket of white before them. Somewhere between the sparkle of snowflakes and the jingling of bells as the horses trotted along, Myra felt an unexplainable pull toward Jeb. It was more than mere attraction to his rugged looks; she was falling for him faster than her impeding heart could refute. Jeb tucked his arm around her as the sleigh glided across the open field.

Was he feeling it too?

At the edge of the rolling acres of land that Jeb owned, he pulled on the reins, bringing the sleigh to a halt. Leaning back, he stared up at the stars, thanking *Gott* for this night and for the beautiful woman who sat nervously beside him. He was nervous too, but he was falling for her—there was no doubt in his mind. It was more than her beauty that attracted him to her; it was the warmth of her spirit that drew him to her with mesmerizing allure.

Jeb turned to her, the moon reflecting in her blue eyes. He pulled off his gloves and cupped his hands over her rosy cheeks, pulling her toward him until his lips met hers. Sweeping his lips over her mouth, he deepened the kiss while she matched his enthusiasm. There was no turning back now—he had fallen for her, and his heart would never be the same.

Myra felt shivers of warmth mixing in her bloodstream as Jeb pulled her toward him, capturing her heart with his when their lips touched. The deeper the kiss moved, the deeper her heart fell for him. Feelings of love surged through her as his lips swept over hers with an electric pulse that sent tingles of warmth all the way to her cold toes. Was love at first sight really possible? She'd told herself all day that such a thing was not even feasible, but here she was falling for Jeb deeper than she ever thought imaginable.

Chapter Ten

Myra stood beside Jeb in front of the Bishop waiting for him to declare them married. She felt like a young girl again with a renewed outlook on life. Being a widow had made her feel like a very old, thirty-year-old woman, but now she felt like she was still in her twenties. Once she'd accepted what *Gott* had for her life, she'd realized what a *gut* life she could have for her and Hannah. Now she would have a son, too—and the possibility for future *bopplies.* Whatever *Gott* had in store for their future, Myra was ready to face it with the love of a *gut mann* like Jeb. She was truly blessed in every way, and she felt as though her life was beginning anew.

Jeb held tight to Myra's hand as they walked through the crowd of *familye* and friends that had come to witness their commitment to each other and to *Gott.* He felt like the luckiest *mann* in the community. He was getting a fresh new start with a beautiful woman who warmed his heart with the love he felt for her.

Hannah and Bart came rushing to them, assaulting them with hugs. They couldn't be happier that their parents had finally found love again.

Jeb knelt down, taking each of their hands in his. "*Danki* for your Christmas prayer."

They all smiled happily.

They were now a *familye.*

The end

For automatic entry to all book giveaways, follow me on Facebook at
http://www.facebook.com/SamanthaBayarr

Please continue down the page for
Amish Sugar Crème Pie recipe

Amish Sugar Crème Pie

Recipe

¾ cup white sugar
1/8 tsp salt
2 cups heavy cream
¼ cup brown sugar
¼ cup corn starch
½ cup butter
1 tsp vanilla

- In a saucepan, combine white sugar, salt, and cream
- Bring to boil
- In separate saucepan, combine brown sugar and cornstarch
- Gradually whisk in hot mixture into brown sugar mixture
- Add butter
- Cook over medium heat, whisk constantly until thick (aprox 5 minutes)
- Simmer one minute, then stir in vanilla

- Pour into pie shell and sprinkle with cinnamon/nutmeg mixture
- Bake at 375*F for 25 minutes
- Serve cooled pie

Coming November, 2012
Contains TWO complete stories!

- Snowflakes on Goose Pond
- Snow Angels

SPECIAL Valentine story!
Coming December, 2012

Coming 2013

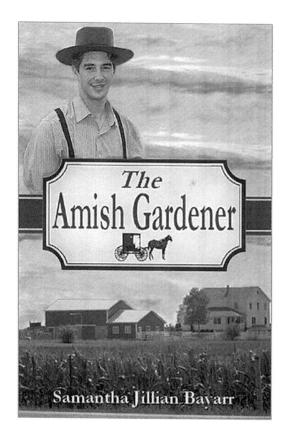

24913038R00085

Printed in Great Britain
by Amazon